The Complete DOG BOOK For Kids

The Complete DOG BOOK For Kids

Official Publication of the
AMERICAN KENNEL CLUB

Howell Book House
New York

Complete, official breed standards are copyrighted by the American Kennel Club and are available by writing to the AKC at 5580 Centerview Drive, Raleigh, NC 27606. They are also published in their entirety in *The Complete Dog Book, 18th Edition*.

New standards, and revisions of standards, are published when approved in the American Kennel Club's official monthly magazine, *AKC Gazette: The Official Journal for the Sport of Purebred Dogs*.

The Complete Dog Book for Kids, 1st Edition

Photographs by Mary Bloom (unless otherwise noted).

Editors:
American Kennel Club:
Noreen E. Baxter—Vice President Public Education and Legislation
Oriol R. Gutierrez, Jr.—Children's Education Coordinator
David Savage—Development Editor
Jan Mahood—Associate Editor
Text Adapted by Antonia LaMotte Gardner from the American Kennel Club's *The Complete Dog Book, 18th Edition*

Howell Book House:
Sean P. Frawley—President & Publisher
Dominique De Vito—Senior Editor
George McKeon—Senior Designer

Special Thanks To:
American Kennel Club:
Mark Threlfall—Director of Special Services
Tilly Grassa—Art Director
Maria Kochanski—Manager of Public Education
Chrissie Diesu—Administrative Assistant

Howell Book House:
Brian Phair—Director of Editorial Services
Denise Hawkins—Production Editor
Felice Primeau—Associate Manager of Marketing and Publicity

Notice:
The Complete Dog Book for Kids is an official publication of the American Kennel Club (AKC). *The Complete Dog Book for Kids* is identified by the AKC seal on the cover and spine.

Howell Book House
A Simon & Schuster Macmillan Company
1633 Broadway
New York, NY 10019

MACMILLAN is a registered trademark of Macmillan, Inc.

Library of Congress Cataloging-in-Publication Data

The complete dog book for kids / official publication of the
American Kennel Club.—1st ed.
           p.   cm.
      Included index.
      ISBN 0–87605–458–0 (hbk.).—ISBN 0–87605–460–2 (pbk.)

      1. Dogs—Juvenile literature.   2. Dog
breeds—Juvenile literature.   3. Dogs—Health—Juvenile
literature.   I. American Kennel Club.

SF426.5.C65   1996

636.7'1—dc20

Manufactured in the United States of America
10 9 8 7 6 5 4 3

Contents

Foreword

Welcome to the wonderful world of purebred dogs!

The American Kennel Club (AKC) made *The Complete Dog Book for Kids* especially for kids like you who want to know more about their best friends—their dogs!

The Complete Dog Book for Kids has big, full-color pictures of every AKC-recognized breed. It also uses language that is easy to understand. We made every effort to make a reference book you would enjoy coming back to again and again.

The Complete Dog Book for Kids will answer questions like: Where did different breeds come from? What were the original functions of different breeds? What are the personalities of different breeds? Other topics include basic care and training information, as well as how you and your dog can participate in AKC events.

As you read *The Complete Dog Book for Kids*, understand that owning a purebred dog can be a wonderful experience—and a big responsibility. Every dog—no matter the breed—deserves a responsible owner.

We hope that this is only the beginning of your journey into the world and the sport of purebred dogs. Have fun!

Introduction

The American Kennel Club (AKC) is pleased to present the first edition of *The Complete Dog Book for Kids*. Adapted from the AKC's *The Complete Dog Book*, it has been designed especially for children!

First published in 1929, *The Complete Dog Book* is now the best selling book of all time about dogs. The AKC is very proud of that fact. Trust has been placed in us as the purebred dog authority. With this in mind, and in response to educators' and librarians' requests nationwide, *The Complete Dog Book for Kids* has become a reality.

Educating the public about purebred dogs is a natural extension of our Mission Statement to: "Maintain a registry for purebred dogs and preserve its integrity; sanction dog events that promote interest in, and sustain the process of, breeding for type and function of purebred dogs; take whatever actions necessary to protect and assure the continuation of the sport of purebred dogs."

It is the last part of the AKC Mission Statement that leads us to share how purebred dogs bring value and joy to our lives. Only by doing so can we be certain that purebred dogs will have a bright future ahead.

Reaching out to children is an important part of our outreach efforts. We hope *The Complete Dog Book for Kids* will help educate children about responsible dog ownership, in addition to introducing them to the world of purebred dogs. We know that informed children will be more likely to become responsible dog owners as adults.

Every effort has been made to be as thorough as possible. All the important topics have been covered in a manner that we hope kids, as well as adults, can easily understand and appreciate.

The Complete Dog Book for Kids is not meant to replace *The Complete Dog Book*. Instead, we view *The Complete Dog Book* as the proud parent of *The Complete Dog Book for Kids*, intended to appeal to a younger audience, providing much of the same information as its parent. For more detailed information, *The Complete Dog Book* remains the AKC's primary source.

We encourage you to use *The Complete Dog Book for Kids* as the start of your exploration into the wonderful world of purebred dogs. Enjoy!

The Complete DOG BOOK For Kids

Part **1**

Dogs
and the
American
Kennel Club

Chapter 1

Before You Buy a Dog

Finding just the dog for you may be time-consuming, but it's worth it in the long run—for you and your dog. *(American Staffordshire Terrier)*

The average dog lives from six to sixteen years or more. That means if you get a puppy or young dog when you are young, that dog could still be a part of your family well past your high school years.

THE RESPONSIBILITIES

You are the center of your dog's universe. He depends on you for just about everything. A young dog needs to be house-trained. He needs to be fed, given water, and exercised every day. He needs to be taken to a veterinarian at least once a year for a checkup and shots.

Unless showing or breeding is in the plans, the dog should be neutered or spayed, preferably in the first year. When the family goes on vacation, or even just away for an overnight visit, arrangements will need to be made for the dog. And every dog should be given at least one course of obedience training.

THE REWARDS

All those responsibilities are balanced by the wonderful experience of living with a dog. Is there anything more appealing and full of bounce and love than a puppy? In less than a year, he won't look like a puppy anymore, but he'll still be lovable and fun. By that time,

The responsibilities of a dog are balanced by the wonderful experience of living with one. *(Borzoi)*

you'll know you've got somebody at home who is always ready to play with you and be your buddy. He'll look up to you as a Very Important Person.

Dogs make sure people keep their sense of humor. They forgive you completely—even when you're wrong. They keep you busy when you're bored and keep you company when you feel like just sitting around doing nothing. When you've provided a dog the sort of life he deserves, taking care of his needs and showing him lots of attention and love, the two of you will form a bond of friendship and trust that will last forever.

THE RIGHT TIME

You're ready for a dog when:

- Everyone in the family wants a dog. A child cannot assume all of the responsibility for a dog. If anyone in the family has allergies, check with a doctor before getting a dog.

- You have enough time for the dog. Walking, exercise, training, feeding, brushing, and playing—not to mention cleaning up after—are all part of dog ownership.

You and your dog will form a bond of friendship and trust that will last forever. *(Spinone Italiano)*

- You have enough space for the sort of dog you want. If space is a factor in your decision, be sure you choose a breed that isn't going to be too big or too active for your space when he's fully grown.

- The family can afford the food, equipment (crate, fencing, etc.), and veterinary care, as well as the initial fee to obtain the dog.

YOUR SORT OF DOG

While choosing a friend for life is a big challenge, there are some practical decisions to make that will help you get started. Think about what sort of temperament, size, gender, coat, and age would fit in with your family. Then, with that general idea in mind, spend some time learning about the various breeds. Talk to breeders, trainers, veterinarians, and owners about their dogs. Visiting special events such as dog shows and field trials will give you firsthand views of specific breeds. The breed descriptions in this book provide helpful information for making your choice.

You're ready for a dog if you have enough time to consistently walk, train, feed, and care for him. *(Collie)*

Temperament

This is the most important trait to consider when selecting a dog: his personality. Here are some questions to keep in mind.

- All dogs need attention, but do I want an active dog to run and play with, or a quiet dog that doesn't require much exercise?

- All dogs must be trained, but am I strong and confident enough to set and keep the rules with a big, bold dog, or am I more suited to a sensitive dog that will respond to gentle training and a low voice?

- Do I want my dog to be super-friendly with everyone he meets, or might a more independent and dignified dog be best for me?

- Fun-loving and smart dogs are sometimes mischievous. How would I handle a dog that just naturally got into digging in the yard or one that barked a lot? Am I willing to work on improving behavior? Am I patient enough to keep reminding my dog of the rules, or do I need a quick learner?

Think about the qualities you want in a dog, then learn about the different breeds to see which fit your lifestyle. *(Schipperke)*

Small, Medium, or Large

That doesn't mean the puppy size, of course, but the grown-up, adult size. Can your house and yard handle a medium or large dog? Some small dogs do need room to run; others are content in pint-sized settings.

Male or Female

If you plan to show or breed your dog, keep in mind that females come into heat approximately twice a year. During this time, they will need to be kept away from other dogs for a week or so. Some unneutered males may go wandering in search of females in heat. In some of the bolder dog breeds, males may be quicker to get into arguments than females. For dogs that are spayed or neutered, these are usually not considerations. A breeder can tell you what male or female personality traits his breed has.

If you like a large, fairly active dog with long hair, the English Setter may be right for you.

Long-Haired or Short

Most dogs shed, and all dogs must be brushed and groomed to stay healthy and happy. A tangled or matted coat makes a dog uncomfortable and irritable. The amount of grooming needed, however, varies from breed to breed. Many dogs have coats of two layers: a soft undercoat with a longer outercoat. Dogs with single coats have less hair to shed but may need protective warm or water-repellent coats in winter and wet weather. Longer coats usually require extra time or expense to keep neat and shiny.

Puppy or Adult

The advantage of getting a puppy is that you'll be able to raise him your own way from the beginning. Puppies are irresistibly cute, but they also need the most time—for house-training, feeding, and handling. Positive interaction with people is critical to the normal development of a puppy. Very

Educate yourself about your breed's health, and keep appointments with the vet. *(Rottweiler)*

Responsible breeders care about the puppies they sell for the dogs' whole lives, and are people you can turn to for advice. *(Golden Retriever)*

young children might have difficulty playing gently with a wriggly puppy. And it will be more work for a busy parent. In these cases, a dog past the puppy stage might fit into the family better. If you plan to show your dog, an older puppy or young adult may display the desired qualities for competition. And remember, even if you get a mature, settled dog, old dogs *can* learn new tricks.

YOUR DOG'S HEALTH

Some breeds may be prone to hereditary diseases or conditions. Check with your sources to see if the breed you like should come with a health certification or has special health needs. You can still be interested in the breed, but you'll be able to avoid problems if you're educated about the breed's health considerations.

WHERE TO GO TO GET A DOG

Once you've figured out the sort of dog you'd like, it's time to contact some breeders. They are the experts in their particular breed. Each breed is represented by a national organization, or club, and many have a rescue club for dogs of that breed that are looking for a new family. You may have to wait for puppies to become available.

Breeders

A responsible breeder should have a clean and orderly kennel. You may ask to see the facilities and to meet one or both parents of the puppies. Make sure the puppy has had interaction with people from his earliest days. "AKC reg" next to a kennel's name means only that no other kennel may use that name in registering or showing dogs with the American Kennel Club. The AKC does not license or approve kennels.

These are some questions to ask a breeder:

- How big will the dog get?

- How old will he be before he acts like an adult dog?

HOW TO REGISTER YOUR DOG WITH THE AKC

- You should receive an AKC application from the breeder (or other seller) partly filled out by the breeder.
- You fill out the rest of the application and, with the application fee, mail it to the AKC.
- Sometimes the dog is eligible for registration, but the seller doesn't have the application. Then the seller must give you a statement, which he or she has signed, containing the following information:

1. Breed, gender, and color of the dog
2. Date of birth of the dog
3. Registered names of the dog's mother and father
4. Name of the breeder

If any problems are encountered, you should write to the AKC at 5580 Centerview Drive, Raleigh, NC 27606.

- How protective is the dog?

- Does the dog have special grooming needs?

- How does he get along with other animals (cats, hamsters, etc.)?

- How long can he be left alone at home?

- Is this dog adaptable to life in the city?

- How much exercise does the dog need, and how often?

- What are the best training methods for this dog?

- What possible health problems might this dog develop?

A breeder should also show interest in the future of the dog by asking you questions. He or she should be available to answer your questions now and long after you've gotten the dog home.

You can find a breeder through dog clubs in your area, through dog obedience trainers, through a veterinarian, or through someone who has a dog of the same breed. The AKC can put you in contact with the national club for your desired breed. You can write the American Kennel Club at 5580 Centerview Drive, Raleigh, NC 27606, (919) 233-9767. From the national club, you can get names of breeders close to you.

SELECTING YOUR PUPPY

Puppies should be eight weeks old or more before leaving their mother. By that age they're weaned off her milk and are ready for puppy food. They've also had critical time with her and their littermates to learn about canine behaviors.

Any puppy you choose should be healthy and alert. Puppies should not be too thin or have runny eyes or noses. Buy only from breeders whose puppies are properly cared for. Visit their kennels to make sure of this.

Often, among healthy puppies, there is one who comes straight up to you first. This is not because he is picking you out, as people often believe. It is because he is the boldest, most outgoing pup in the litter. If that is the

Even a nice dog may try to protect himself with a growl and a nip at certain times. Biting is a dog's natural way of protecting himself. Since dogs sometimes see kids as equals, they may try to send them a warning, doggy-style, when things get tense. Here's how to avoid misunderstandings with your own or anyone else's dog.

- Always ask a dog's owner if you may pet the dog.

There may be a very good reason why a dog should not be touched. He may be "on duty" as a handicapped person's assistance dog, or he may be injured, ill, or afraid of children.

- Approach a dog from the front or side.

Hold your hands low and speak softly. Surprising a dog from behind or forcing him into a corner may cause him to snap in fear. Waving hands in the air or screaming may overexcite him, causing him to snap in fear or even in play.

- Let a dog eat in peace.

If there's one place a dog may get defensive, it's at the food dish. Your dog shouldn't growl when you get near his dish, but you shouldn't interfere with his eating.

- Watch out for special toys.

Some dogs have powerful feelings for their balls or chew toys. Never take a bone or toy from a dog's mouth unless you have trained him to drop it and give it to you first.

- Avoid teasing, rough wrestling, or tug-of-war games.

Dogs may get too enthusiastic in these sorts of games and forget you're not a dog. Fetch, Frisbee, hide and seek, agility courses, and flyball are better outlets for your dog's energy.

- Respect a dog's space.

Dogs naturally defend their territories. Sticking your hand inside a strange dog's pen or in a car window where a dog is sitting may put him in a defensive situation and he might bite to protect his territory.

- Leave fighting dogs alone.

Do not try to break up a dogfight! Most fights end quickly, but it's a good idea to remain quiet and get an adult who can stop the fight with a garden hose or lemon juice in a squirt bottle. Trying to separate or yelling at fighting dogs makes them more excited, and they might turn on you.

- Observe dog body language.

Dogs normally resort to biting only when they think you haven't listened to their warnings. Watch out for a dog who is barking, growling, or showing his teeth. Beware if his ears are back, legs stiff, tail up, or hair standing up on his back. Slowly walk away and say "No" firmly, arms by your side. Do not scream, stare into his eyes, or run away. If you run, he will chase you and may attack.

- Tell your friends what you know.

When friends come to your house, introduce them to your dog and explain the house rules. When you're out, share your knowledge. The more everyone knows about dogs, the better world it will be for dogs and for people.

personality you want, there's your puppy. One may be hiding shyly in the corner. This puppy may be the sensitive one of the bunch. If he is from a sensitive breed, maybe he would be happiest in a gentle, quiet family.

The puppy who lets you play with him, who lets you pick him up without struggling too much, and who seems happy, healthy, and clean is most likely

When choosing a pup, look for one who lets you play with him and who is confident and content, without extremes. *(Golden Retreiver)*

It's wonderful to have your dog friend at home. *(Labrador Retreiver)*

going to be typical of his breed, without extremes at one end or the other of the behavior scale. The rest will depend on you and how you raise the dog.

BRINGING PUPPY HOME

When it's time to bring home your dog, before you leave the breeder get written instructions on feeding and when the dog needs to go to the veterinarian. The breeder may recommend a vet, or you can ask a friend who has a dog or cat what veterinarian he or she goes to. It's best to choose a veterinarian who is not too far away or inconvenient to visit. That way, you'll be more likely to keep those important appointments. (A new puppy or dog should be taken right away to your vet to check his general health.)

Finally, papers for AKC registration should be filled out with the breeder. Your dog must be registered to participate in AKC events. "AKC registered" means your dog is listed in the records of the AKC as a purebred dog. You will then be able to research the complete history of your dog's family, and your dog will become part of the breed's official registry.

What is the American Kennel Club?

The American Kennel Club has celebrated the partnership of human and dog since the club's formation in 1884. *(Welsh Springer Spaniel)*

The American Kennel Club (AKC) was formed in 1884 to advance the interests of purebred dogs. The AKC is a nonprofit organization whose mission is carried out in part through canine health research, public education, and programs to protect dogs and preserve the rights of their owners.

The AKC employs more than 500 people who work on matters related to the study, breeding, showing, health, and welfare of purebred dogs. AKC employees are dedicated to helping you become a well-informed, responsible dog owner so that you and your dog can enjoy each other and others can enjoy you and your dog.

The AKC, which recognizes over 140 breeds, has the largest purebred dog registry in the world. Each year, more than a million new dogs are registered.

Where *are* all these dogs? Many are with their human companions who belong to one or more of the 4,500 dog clubs affiliated with the AKC. These dogs and their owners take part in some of the more than 13,000 AKC-approved events a year, including conformation shows; obedience trials; performance events such as hunting tests, field trials, tracking, lure coursing, and agility; and educational programs.

A healthy dog is an ideal companion. (*Miniature Pinscher*)

FOR THE WELFARE OF PUREBRED DOGS

Scientific Advances

In 1995 the AKC established the *AKC Canine Health Foundation* to fund research and provide educational programs dealing with breeding healthy dogs. Scientists conduct research to learn new ways to cure disease. Scientists also develop ways to test dogs for the presence of defective genes—genes that don't work right—and to breed puppies that don't have those genes. The AKC also sponsors conferences for scientists and breeders.

The *AKC Canine Health Foundation* emphasizes the understanding of dog genetics, since its primary focus is on healthy dogs. Of course, much research deals with DNA and molecular genetics, since DNA is the hereditary material. The interest in genetics extends from certain disorders—such as blindness—all the way to instincts and behavior, such as herding and retrieving, which are unique to the dog world.

Veterinarian Studies Program

A *Veterinarian Studies Program* gives scholarships to students who want to study companion animals in veterinary school. These students go on to become the veterinarians and researchers of tomorrow.

Recovering Lost Dogs

The *AKC Companion Animal Recovery Program* helps dog owners find their lost animals. This 24-hour-a-day nationwide pet identification and recovery service has a central database that records identification numbers for dog owners who have tattooed or microchipped their dogs (two means of identification in addition to the dog tag). If someone finds the dog, he can contact the AKC. If the dog is on the AKC list, the owner is notified that his dog has been found!

Dogs and the Law

The AKC also works toward passage of laws that protect the rights of dog owners. *The Canine Legislation Department* works with local and regional

These are just some of the brochures on dog care the AKC publishes.

The *AKC Gazette* and *Events Calendar* are published monthly.

dog organizations to make sure that new laws are fair, can be enforced, and do not discriminate against dogs.

Educating the Public

Public Education is a national program that promotes responsible dog ownership. More than 3,200 public education coordinators from dog clubs work with the AKC to educate their communities about dogs and dog ownership.

In the *Best Friends* program, dogs and their owners visit 30,000 elementary schools each year.

The *Canine Ambassador Program* is one in which local dog clubs give demonstrations in schools. Many "ambassadors" use the *Taking Care of Corey* program, which includes an animated video, to teach young children about the responsibilities of owning a dog. Unofficial "ambassadors" are young people who teach in their communities what they've learned about dogs in their own AKC classroom programs.

Speaking Out for Dogs

Dogs can't speak for themselves, so the AKC speaks for them. The *Public Relations Department* gives information about purebred dogs and AKC activities to newspapers, television stations, and other news sources. It produces brochures that tell about the AKC and organizes events to introduce new programs. The *Club Educational Services Department* takes the AKC booth, with its videos and publications, to major dog shows. When you attend a dog show, you can learn about the AKC by visiting this booth and talking with the people there.

The *Publishing Department* tells the story of purebred dogs in print. The *AKC Gazette*, a monthly magazine, is full of information about purebred dogs. Stories about all aspects of dogs and dog people are illustrated with full-color photographs. There are regular columns

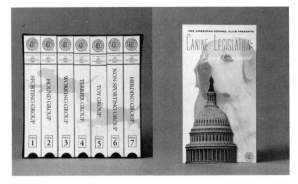

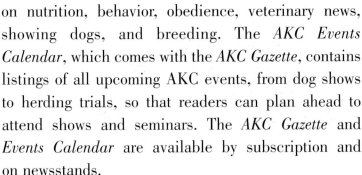

on nutrition, behavior, obedience, veterinary news, showing dogs, and breeding. The *AKC Events Calendar*, which comes with the *AKC Gazette*, contains listings of all upcoming AKC events, from dog shows to herding trials, so that readers can plan ahead to attend shows and seminars. The *AKC Gazette* and *Events Calendar* are available by subscription and on newsstands.

The AKC also publishes *Puppies* magazine, which is sent to owners of newly registered puppies. As the name implies, it contains information on every aspect of puppy care.

The AKC offers a wide selection of books on purebred dogs. *The Complete Dog Book for Kids* and *The Complete Dog Book* are official publications of the AKC, as is *American Kennel Club Dog Care and Training*. The Communications Division oversees the production of numerous videos on individual breeds, training, performance events, and responsible dog ownership.

A selection of videos produced by the American Kennel Club.

CLUBS FOR DOGS

Every breed recognized by the AKC has a national or "parent" club. For example, the Golden Retriever Club of America is the parent club for local and regional Golden Retriever clubs all over the country. These clubs *are*, in essence, the AKC because delegates from the clubs help make AKC rules and elect AKC directors from among the member clubs. The AKC recognizes eleven types of clubs:

All-breed

Specialty (single breed)

Obedience

Tracking

Kids—and dogs—can learn a lot from the AKC's book on care and training. (*Golden Retriever*)

All-breed clubs host dog shows across the country.
(French Bulldog)

Field trial

Hunting test

Herding

Coonhound

Lure coursing

Agility

Earthdog

Approximately 4,500 affiliated clubs, of which more than 500 are member clubs, hold AKC events and use AKC information to conduct dog shows, performance events, educational programs, training classes, and health clinics. Some clubs also find good homes for unwanted and abandoned dogs through their *Breed Rescue Programs*.

This network of dog-smart people across the country can help you choose a dog that is right for you and your family. And once you have that special dog, the clubs can continue to be a good source of information and fun-filled activities for you and your new friend. To find out about clubs in your area, contact AKC Customer Service, 5580 Centerview Drive, Raleigh, NC 27606 (919) 233-9767.

THE AKC LIBRARY

The AKC library contains more than sixteen thousand books. It is one of the largest dog libraries in the world. On its shelves you can find this year's very latest books as well as many rare books, one of which is over four hundred years old. The library also boasts a world-famous art collection with works by renowned dog painters and sculptors.

More than one thousand people a year from all over the world visit the library to study every known breed of dog in books, magazines, pictures, videos, and in issues of the *AKC Gazette* going back to 1889. In the library they can also admire portraits of the beautiful dogs that belonged to kings and queens, farmers, sportsmen, shepherds, and peasants. The library is housed in AKC headquarters in New York City and is open to the public weekdays from 9:30 A.M. until 4:00 P.M.

THE DOG MUSEUM

Organized by the American Kennel Club Foundation, the Dog Museum of America was the first public museum for the display and study of canine art. The museum, originally located in New York City and affiliated with the AKC, opened in 1982. In 1987, it was renamed the Dog Museum, became independent and moved from its original New York location to the historic Jarville House in St. Louis, Missouri. In 1995, the Dog Museum reaffiliated with the AKC.

Among its treasures are gallery after gallery of purebred portraits by the outstanding dog artists of America, England, and continental Europe. Besides a permanent collection of treasures, special exhibits celebrate the dog in its many roles. Recently, "Dogs of War," showed how many breeds of dogs served our country in World Wars I and II, the Korean War, and the Vietnam War.

Chapter 3

The Sport of Dogs

More than thirteen thousand events drawing two million entries are held each year under American Kennel Club rules. Dog shows, obedience trials, agility, herding, tracking, field trials, hunting tests, lure coursing, and earthdog tests are designed for dogs of every breed and inclination. You and your dog can participate in these as well as Junior Showmanship and the Canine Good Citizen program. Let's look at all these "sports" of dogs.

DOG SHOWS

Dog shows are some of the most popular ways to compete in the sport of dogs. *(Non-Sporting Group)*

At dog shows, judges evaluate a dog's *conformation*, or how closely his physical structure *conforms* to his particular breed's "standard." A standard is a detailed description of a breed written by that breed's parent club.

Breed standards describe exactly how an ideal dog of each breed should look and act. Once written, standards are approved by the AKC board of directors. Most breeds' standards were written and approved many years ago but have undergone variations and updates over the years. This book contains excerpts from each breed's standard; the complete standards are available from the parent clubs of the breeds or from the AKC.

In the show ring, the judge should select the dog that comes closest to the breed standard. The judge looks at:

- General appearance—size, proportion, and substance

- Head—expression, eyes, ears, skull, muzzle, and bite

Dogs are judged by how well they compare to the standards for their breeds. *(Golden Retriever)*

- Neck, topline, body (including tail)

- Forequarters

- Hindquarters

- Coat

- Color

- Gait—how the dog moves coming, going, and from the side

- Temperament

All these things contribute to the overall dog, and it is up to the judge to choose which dog he or she thinks is the winner.

Dog shows can be specialized events featuring a certain breed (specialty show) or include all breeds (all-breed show). At a specialty show, dogs of only one breed compete against each other for Best of Breed. At an all-breed show, dogs of many breeds compete against each other for Best in Show, though each breed competes within its own breed until the final classes.

Dogs and their handlers go through a process of elimination in dog shows. Most are working toward the 15 points needed for a championship title. That takes several wins over the course of several shows. Dogs winning in formal "licensed" or "point shows" earn points toward championships or credits toward titles.

Here's how an all-breed show works:

First Level: Classes

Dogs are separated by breed, then by gender. Males are called dogs, and females are called bitches. Dogs and bitches of each breed are then divided into the following classes:

Puppy

Novice

Bred by Exhibitor

American-Bred

Open

The judge selects a first-, second-, third- and fourth-place winner from each class.

It's a very special dog who makes it to the higher levels of dog-show classes.

Second Level: Winners and Reserve Winners

All the class winners then go into the Winners class for bitches or Winners class for dogs. From all the male class winners, one is selected to be the Winners Dog. From the class-winning females, one is named Winners Bitch. In case something should happen to disqualify the Winners Dog or Winners Bitch, the judge also selects runners-up called the Reserve Winners Dog and the Reserve Winners Bitch from the Winners classes. The second-place dog and bitch from the first-level classes come back into the ring so that the judge can make the Reserve selections. The two Winners receive points toward their championships.

Third Level: Best of Breed, Best of Opposite Sex and Best of Winners

At this level the competition is stiffer than ever. Dogs and bitches who have already earned their champion title at other shows compete with the Winners Dog and Winners Bitch from this show for the Best of Breed title. Males and females compete against each other for this coveted award.

After selecting Best of Breed, the judge makes two other awards at this level: He chooses Best of Opposite Sex to the Best of Breed winner (so if Best of Breed is a dog, Best of Opposite Sex would be a bitch and vice versa), and he chooses Best of Winners from the male and female Winners of level two.

Fourth Level: Groups

At all-breed shows, the next category brings together the Best of Breed winners from all the breeds. The breeds are sorted by Groups, of which there are seven: Sporting, Hound, Working, Terrier, Toy, Non-Sporting, and Herding. All the Best of Breed winners from the Sporting Group compete against each other, and so on. In each Group, first, second, third, and fourth places are awarded. The first-place winners of each Group move up to the next and final level.

The top seven dogs—the Group winners—compete for the ultimate prize: Best in Show. At the largest all-breed shows, one winner triumphs over thousands of competitors—all in only a day or two! No matter what size the entry, winning Best in Show is an incomparable thrill for you and your dog.

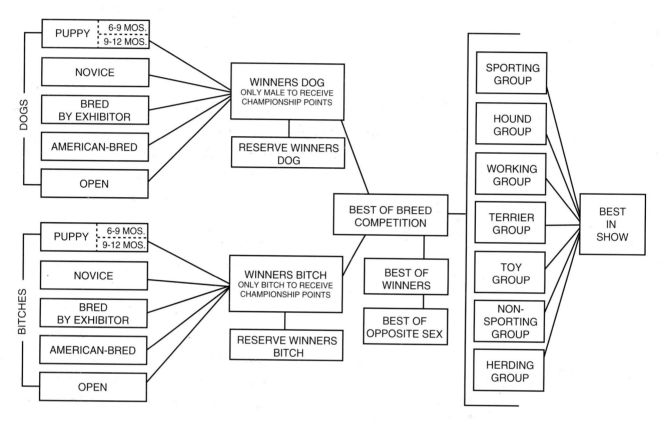

AKC'S PERFORMANCE EVENTS

Performance events give today's purebred dogs the opportunity to perform the tasks for which they were originally bred. Aside from obedience and agility trials, in which all breeds participate, various performance events are open only to those breeds developed to perform specific tasks, such as hunting, lure coursing, herding, or going to ground.

Obedience Trials

In obedience trials, you and your dog work together as a team. Your dog must perform a set of exercises which the judge scores. The dog's conformation has nothing to do with his ability to perform in obedience. Even spayed and neutered dogs may compete.

This Borzoi retrieves the dumbbell as part of an Open obedience class.

Obedience is divided into three levels, each more difficult than the one before. Your dog earns a title for each level completed. The levels are on the left and the titles earned for them are on the right:

Novice—Companion Dog (CD)

Open—Companion Dog Excellent (CDX)

Utility—Utility Dog (UD)

Dogs that have completed their UD title can compete for the Utility Dog Excellent (UDX) title or Obedience Trial Champion (OTCh).

Novice. In novice work, your dog learns six exercises to help him be a good companion. They are heel on lead, stand for examination, heel free, recall, long sit, and long down.

Open work consists of seven exercises: heel free, drop on recall, retrieve on flat, retrieve over the high jump, broad jump, long sit, and long down.

Utility work consists of five advanced exercises: a signal exercise, two scent-discrimination tests, directed retrieve, directed jumping, and group examination.

Your dog must earn three "legs" to receive an obedience title. To get credit for a leg, he must score at least 170 points of a possible 200 and get more than 50 percent on each exercise.

Agility Trials

In agility trials, your dog and you demonstrate that you can work together through a variety of situations. Your dog will probably think that this work is more like play! He will go over jumps, weave through poles, run through a tunnel, climb up and down an A-frame, jump through a tire, and negotiate various other structures as you run alongside, urging him on.

This program begins with basic entry-level agility and progresses to more complex levels. It keeps your dog (and you) in condition and is great fun.

A tire jump is just one of the obstacles your dog will have to navigate on an agility course. (Alaskan Malamute)

To participate in AKC agility, a dog needs to be at least twelve months old and registered with the AKC either officially, with an Indefinite Listing Privilege (ILP) number, or with AKC Limited Registration. Spayed and neutered dogs are also eligible. At each level, there are classes for all sizes of dogs from the smallest, like Chihuahuas, to the tallest, like Irish Wolfhounds.

At each level, your dog must pass the test three times under two different judges before earning the title and moving up to the next level. For the Master Agility Excellent title, the dog must pass the test at the Agility Excellent level 10 times. Titles your dog can earn in agility are:

Novice Agility (NA)

Open Agility (OA)

Agility Excellent (AX)

Master Agility Excellent (MX)

Tracking

Tracking tests held under AKC regulations require a dog to follow a trail by scent. He must find articles placed on the track, retrieve them, and return them to the judges. A dog earns titles in tracking by passing a series of tests that increase in difficulty. Some of the most difficult tests challenge a dog to follow human scent across various surfaces and through changing conditions. Tracking titles are:

Tracking Dog (TD)

Tracking Dog Excellent (TDX)

Variable Surface Tracking Test (VST)

Champion Tracker (CT)

Janice Raines

Judith Strom

Field Trials and Hunting Tests

Field trials demonstrate a sporting dog's ability to perform the tasks for which his breed was developed—to find game. They are held separately for the pointing breeds, retrievers, and spaniels, as well as Beagles, Basset Hounds, and Dachshunds. Retrievers, pointing breeds, and spaniels are also eligible to participate in hunting tests. The difference between field trials and hunting tests is that in field trials the dogs are judged against each other; in hunting tests the dogs are judged against a standard of performance for the breed, so they are less competitive. Both events are demanding, and dogs are evaluated at increasingly difficult levels.

Field trial titles are:

Field Champion (FC)

Amateur Field Champion (AFC)

Hunting test titles are:

Junior Hunter (JH)

Senior Hunter (SH)

Master Hunter (MH)

Herding

The herding program is divided into testing and trial sections. The herding program begins with testing the general herding ability of the dogs. The less experienced dogs can earn the Herding Tested (HT) title if they show that they have an inborn herding ability and are trainable in herding.

Dogs that have already had some training in herding compete for the Pre-Trial Tested (PT) title. They herd a small group of animals through a simple course to earn the title.

After the testing level, the dogs move on to the more difficult trial levels. Dogs compete for the Herding Started (HS), then the Herding Intermediate (HI), and finally the Herding Excellent (HX) titles.

Once they have earned their HX title, the dogs take part in even more difficult exercises in herding. They must prove that they can herd different kinds of animals, including uncooperative ones, in a variety of settings. Three different courses test their abilities. Those who can win 15 points earn a Herding Championship (HCh).

The herding titles are:

Herding Tested (HT)

Pre-Trial Tested (PT)

Herding Started (HS)

Herding Intermediate (HI)

Herding Excellent (HX)

Herding Champion (HCh)

Lure Coursing

Lure coursing tests sighthounds on their abilities to hunt down prey by sight— the purpose for which these breeds were developed. In these competitions, the dogs must chase the prey (plastic bags), sometimes by traveling long distances. They are judged for overall ability, following, speed, agility, and endurance. The titles they can earn are:

Junior Courser (JC)

Senior Courser (SC)

Field Champion (FC)

Earthdog Tests

This event is for small terriers and Dachshunds. It tests the natural abilities of these dogs to hunt for prey (also known as quarry) by going to ground (into burrows or tunnels). After all, terriers got their name from the word *terra,* which means "ground" in Latin. Spayed and neutered dogs are permitted in this event.

In Introduction to Quarry, no title is awarded and dogs with no training can participate. Two rats, safe in a cage, are placed in a long, narrow tunnel in the ground. Dogs must find the quarry within three minutes and then must show interest in catching it by digging, growling, or barking at it. The earthdog titles are:

Junior Earthdog (JE)

Senior Earthdog (SE)

Master Earthdog (ME)

MORE ABOUT TITLES

Once your dog has earned a title, the title becomes part of his official record forever. It is added to the dog's listing in the AKC registry and is included in the registration papers that belong to you, his owner.

Some titles, called prefixes, are listed in front of the dog's name. Others, the suffixes, come after the name. To help you understand a dog's papers, here are the titles with their abbreviations:

Breed, Obedience, Herding, and Lure Coursing Titles (Prefixes)

Ch	Champion	**HCh**	Herding Champion
FC	Field Champion (Field Trial/Lure Coursing)	**DC**	Dual Champion (Ch and FC)
AFC	Amateur Field Champion	**TC**	Triple Champion (Ch, FC, and OTCh)
OTCh	Obedience Trial Champion		

Obedience, Hunting, Herding, and Lure Coursing Titles (Suffixes)

CD	Companion Dog	**MH**	Master Hunter
CDX	Companion Dog Excellent	**HT**	Herding Tested
UD	Utility Dog	**PT**	Pre-Trial Tested
NA	Novice Agility	**HS**	Herding Started
OA	Open Agility	**HI**	Herding Intermediate
AX	Agility Excellent	**HX**	Herding Excellent
MX	Master Agility Excellent	**JC**	Junior Courser
TD	Tracking Dog	**SC**	Senior Courser
TDX	Tracking Dog Excellent	**JE**	Junior Earthdog
JH	Junior Hunter	**SE**	Senior Earthdog
SH	Senior Hunter	**ME**	Master Earthdog

Chapter 4

You and Your Dog

Your dog is eager to work and learn with you.
(German Wirehaired Pointer)

Dogs that work and play with people and other dogs lead happy lives. Their human companions have fun, too. As you work with your dog, your dog will teach you things: concentration, teamwork, consistency, patience, and the joy of accomplishment. Because dogs love to be with you and are eager to please, your activities together are the basis for your best-friendship.

No matter what breed of dog you own, the AKC has an event that will give your dog the opportunity to work with you and to shine in the activity for which his breed was developed. You and your dog can receive recognition in the form of ribbons, trophies, and titles—or simply enjoy the pleasure of learning and performing together.

PROGRAMS FOR KIDS AND DOGS

The AKC has two special programs for kids and their dogs: Junior Showmanship and the Canine Good Citizen® (CGC) program. Of course kids may compete in the other AKC activities described in chapter 3, "The Sport of Dogs," and adults can compete in Canine Good Citizen®, but CGC—and especially Junior Showmanship—are the perfect places for kids to enter the sport of dogs.

Junior Showmanship

In Junior Showmanship, you'll be judged on how well you show your dog. *(Chow Chow)*

Junior Showmanship classes at dog shows are judged only on the ability of the junior to handle the dog. The conformation or quality of the dog is not judged. This competition for kids age 10 through 18 encourages young people to participate in the sport of dogs. It provides junior handlers with an opportunity to compete, learn, practice, and improve their skills and sportsmanship. And finally, it prepares them for lives as handlers, judges, veterinarians, dog writers, trainers, breeders, show superintendents, canine health researchers—and responsible dog owners.

There are countless opportunities in the sport of dogs for young people who combine a love of dogs with the desire to work hard and learn. The successful juniors of today will set the tone for the sport in the 21st century.

The Junior Showmanship Classes

The first of two classes in Junior Showmanship is called Novice, and it's for first-time competitors or those who haven't qualified for Open. The second is Open, for juniors who have won three first places in Novice classes. Novice and Open classes are sometimes divided by age: Juniors are at least 10 and under 14 years old and seniors are at least 14 and under 18.

In the Junior Showmanship classes, the judge evaluates the juniors in four basic areas: proper breed presentation, skill in presenting the individual's dog, knowledge of ring procedures, and appearance and conduct. Competitors are asked to:

- Move the dog with the rest of the class.

- Present the dog in the proper standing position and use an examining table if the breed is normally judged on a table.

- Move the dog individually in a regular pattern.

At the end of the classes, all winners compete for the title of Best Junior Handler.

What Judges Look For

Juniors should know how things work in the show ring. They should be familiar with the terms for what they'll need to do ("Out and back," for example) and should be able to follow the judge's directions and make good use of the available space in the ring. Clothes should be comfortable, neat, and appropriate. Juniors should appear confident, prepared, businesslike, and attentive and should be courteous toward the judge and their competitors.

The presentation of the dog is the highlight of the competition. The dog, like the handler, should be clean, neat, and well-groomed. The junior must keep the dog's attention without dramatic or unnecessary motions, move the dog along at the proper speed without distracting or interfering with the judge's view of the dog, and be aware of what is going on in the ring while concentrating on the dog, not the judge or other handlers.

Learning to Show Your Dog

There are many sources of information for juniors eager to learn. Find out about handling classes in your area. Ask your parents, experienced breeders and handlers, and former juniors for advice on the sport of Junior Showmanship. Read books on handling and on individual breeds. Attend as many dog shows as you can and observe the breed and group judging.

The Canine Good Citizen® Program

Dogs live with people, so they need to become good citizens just like the rest of us. Most dogs—like most people—aren't born with perfect manners. They need to be taught how to politely greet strange people and dogs. They need to learn when it's okay to bounce around and when it's not. And they should listen to you at all times. When you say "Come!" it could mean "Get over here and stop jumping on our guest!" Or, in a dangerous situation, this basic command could mean the difference between life and death for your dog.

A Canine Good Citizen® (CGC) gets along with everyone around him—family members, veterinarians, handlers, and even people who aren't used to dogs. Your dog may not be able to say the magic words, "please" and "thank you," but he should know just what to do when you say "come," "heel," "sit," "down," and "stay."

The Canine Good Citizen® program is good for your dog. He will be happy knowing how to please you. Teaching him will strengthen your friendship. If your dog has good manners, everybody else will like him almost as much as you do.

The CGC program helps you teach your dog the basic manners he needs to get along in today's world. When you and your dog can perform all the required exercises, you take a short test. This is not a difficult or formal competition. It is simply 10 exercises for you and your dog. They don't need to be done perfectly, but when they're done properly, you and your dog will receive an official AKC Canine Good Citizen® certificate.

The Canine Good Citizen® Test

Here are the 10 steps your dog must perform to become a Canine Good Citizen.

1. Accepting a Friendly Stranger

This test shows that the dog will allow a friendly stranger to approach him and speak to his owner in a natural, everyday situation. The evaluator and handler shake hands and chat. The dog must show no sign of resentment or shyness and must not break position or try to go to the evaluator.

TRAINING TIP: *While training your dog to stay calm around new people, invite friends to your house and ask them to help you practice this exercise. When you walk your dog, have him sit/stay while you talk to neighbors.*

2. Sitting Politely for Petting

This exercise demonstrates that your dog will remain calm and friendly for a stranger's attentions. While your dog is sitting at your side, the evaluator pets him on the head and body only, then circles you and your dog, completing the test. The dog must not show shyness or resentment.

TRAINING TIP: *To train your dog to receive attention nicely, start by putting him in the sit position. Then let family members, the people he knows best, pet him while keeping him in that sit. When he can do that, try it with other people he knows. With your praise and encouragement, he will soon learn to take attention from strangers with the same grace.*

3. Appearance and Grooming

A neat and tidy appearance shows that a dog is well cared for. This test demonstrates that the dog is well groomed. It also shows that the dog will allow others, such as a veterinarian or a groomer, to handle him. The evaluator checks the dog for a healthy appearance, looking at weight, cleanliness, and alertness. Then the evaluator brushes the dog and lightly examines the ears and each front foot.

TRAINING TIP: *Most dogs love petting and handling. Getting them used to brushing and gentle handling of sensitive areas like ears and feet should start from day one. Then they're less afraid when it's bath or nail-clipping time. If a dog is fearful of such handling, it's best to get him used to it slowly and gradually. Slipping him a few treats while grooming or checking his body makes it more pleasant for him. With loving human contact, shy dogs learn to trust people.*

4. Out for a Walk (Walking on a Loose Lead)

A dog is welcome on neighborhood sidewalks and paths when he walks on his lead beside his owner. This test demonstrates that you are in control of your dog. The dog may be on your left or right side. There is a left turn, a right turn, and an about turn, with at least one stop in between and another at the end. The dog need not be perfectly aligned with you and need not sit when you stop.

TRAINING TIP: *The basics of walking a dog on a lead are covered in obedience training classes. This is a very simple explanation: Hold the end of the lead in your right hand, and with your left hand hold the lead close to your dog's collar so you can control his movements. Practice turns to reinforce your dog's habit of staying close to you. Praise your dog when he's walking close to you and make the experience a pleasant one.*

5. Walking through a Crowd

This exercise demonstrates that your dog can get through a crowd of people while remaining under control. You and your dog walk around and pass close to at least three people. The dog may show some interest in the strangers, but shouldn't be overexuberant, shy, or resentful. You may talk to your dog and

encourage or praise him throughout the test. He should not be straining at the lead.

TRAINING TIP: *If you don't often encounter other people or dogs on your walks, try going into town or visiting playgrounds with your dog. Start by keeping your distance, and go on a day when it's not too crowded. Gradually let the dog get used to being around strangers.*

6. Sit, Down, and Stay on Command

This test shows that the dog has had some training and responds to commands. The dog's lead is replaced with a 20-foot rope or training lead supplied by the evaluator. The owner gives the commands as needed, and the evaluator determines if the dog has responded to the owner. The dog must remain in place, but may change positions, until the evaluator gives the release command.

TRAINING TIP: *The sit, down, and stay commands are essential to the control of a dog. They are learned in obedience training classes, but dogs need to be reminded of these commands. Practice a little every day. Gently guide the dog into position. Stay close beside the dog while he's learning the stay. When he can remain still for one to two minutes in a sit or two to three minutes in a down, add distractions. After that, you can begin moving farther and farther away. If the dog can't hold the stay, move closer and try again. Don't forget the praise and rewards for success.*

7. Coming When Called

This test shows that the dog will come when called by the owner. The dog is on the 20-foot line that was used in step 6. The owner walks 10 feet from the dog, turns to face the dog, and calls him. The owner may tell the dog to stay, or simply walk away. The dog may be in the sit, down, or stand position. If the dog tries to follow the owner, the evaluator may distract the dog by petting, for example, until the owner is 10 feet away. When the dog comes, the owner attaches the dog's own lead.

TRAINING TIP: *What could be easier? The first lesson you teach your dog is to come when called. This should be a regular part of his day from the first day he comes home with you.*

8. Reaction to Another Dog

In this test, the dog shows he can be near another dog and remain calm. With the evaluator watching, two owners with their dogs on leashes approach each other from about 10 yards away. They meet, shake hands, and greet one another casually, then continue on their way for about five yards. The dog being tested should not go to the other dog or the other dog's owner.

TRAINING TIP: *Good places to practice dog-to-dog encounters are veterinary offices, boarding kennels, or grooming establishments. These are important places for your dog to mind his manners around other dogs. Put the dog in a stay whenever another dog passes by. Give the dogs plenty of room to pass one another. The other dog may not be as well trained as your dog.*

9. Reaction to Distractions

This test shows that the dog can remain confident and polite around the normal sounds of the world outside your home. The evaluator will test the dog with a sound distraction (a shout, for example) and a sight distraction (maybe waving a coat in front of the dog). The dog may be curious or surprised but should not try to run away, bark, or show aggression.

TRAINING TIP: *Some dogs are fearful of sudden noises or movements. Start by introducing the distraction at a great distance and give treats and petting along with it. Try dropping a book as a sound distraction or having a friend jog past your dog as a sight distraction. Slowly bring the distraction closer. If the dog shows fear, move the distraction farther away and try again later. Don't get angry with a dog for being afraid, but don't baby him or he won't learn to conquer his fears.*

Some dogs may become aggressive at distractions. Chasing joggers is one example. Correct your dog firmly right away for undesirable behavior, and praise him when he gets it right. With a very bold dog, this may be a job for an adult.

10. Supervised Separation

This test shows that the dog can be left with another person while the owner goes out of sight. The evaluator will say something like "Would you like me to watch your dog?" and hold the dog's six-foot lead while you move out of the

dog's sight. Your dog does not have to stay in position, but he should not bark, whine, howl, pace unnecessarily, or show anything other than mild agitation or nervousness.

Never tie up your dog and leave him while you run an errand. But in an emergency, you may have to ask someone—preferably someone you know—to hold him. This test shows that the dog can handle this situation without panicking or disturbing others.

TRAINING TIP: *You have been learning to trust your dog. Now he must trust you. Working with you has given your dog confidence. He knows that even if you have to leave him with someone else, you'll be back. To get him used to your leaving him, start at home by putting him in the stay position and moving out of sight for a few seconds. Concentrating on the stay keeps his spirits up. When he's used to that, start leaving him with a new command: "Wait here" or "I'll be right back." That means he doesn't have to stay in position but knows that he should wait for you.*

Dog clubs, obedience schools, and other organizations such as community colleges, 4-H, and the scouts may administer a CGC test. The AKC provides information and test kits. If you would like to order the new CGC test, contact the AKC's CGC Department at 5580 Centerview Drive, Raleigh, NC 27606, (919) 233-9767.

Chapter 5

Anatomy and Measuring a Dog

ANATOMY

As you learn more about dogs and more about the individual breeds, you'll learn that the way they are built is crucial to what they can do and how they look. To help you understand how a dog is built, and to familiarize yourself with the terms dog people use to describe dogs, study these anatomical charts. See if you can find the same points on your dog!

The Dog's Anatomy

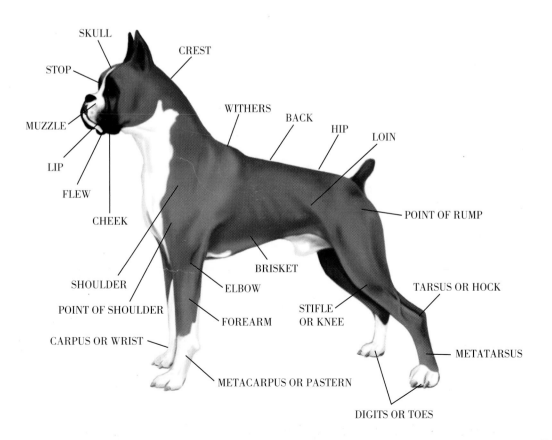

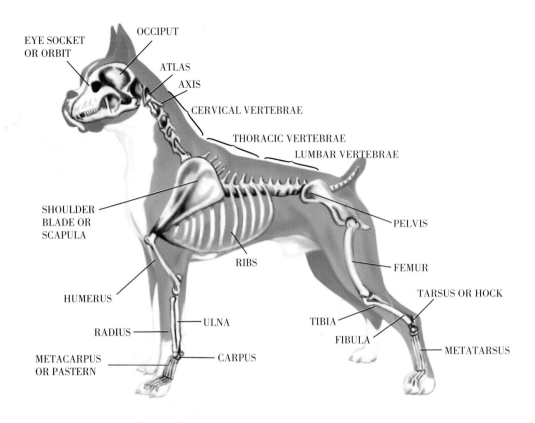

EYE SOCKET
OR ORBIT

OCCIPUT

ATLAS

AXIS

CERVICAL VERTEBRAE

THORACIC VERTEBRAE

LUMBAR VERTEBRAE

SHOULDER
BLADE OR
SCAPULA

PELVIS

RIBS

FEMUR

HUMERUS

TARSUS OR HOCK

ULNA

TIBIA

RADIUS

FIBULA

METATARSUS

METACARPUS
OR PASTERN

CARPUS

MEASURING HEIGHT AND LENGTH

It is often a disqualifying fault for a particular breed to be shorter or taller than the standard requires. For this reason, owners need to measure their dogs to see where the dogs "fit" according to the standard, and judges often carry wickets, or measuring instruments, with them in the ring in case they want to measure a dog. How tall and long is your dog?

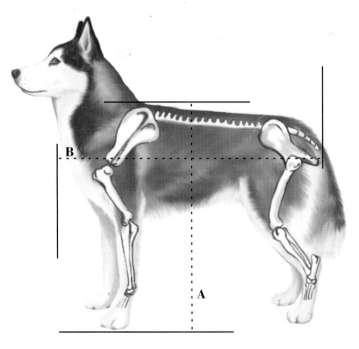

Height is measured from a point horizontal with the withers straight down to the ground (line A). Length is measured from point of shoulder to point of buttock (line B).

Part 2

AKC-
Recognized
Breeds,
by Group

SPORTING DOGS

These dogs were developed over the years to work closely with people hunting birds. The various pointers, retrievers, setters, and spaniels are all in the Sporting Group. Each has a specialty. Pointers find the game and show the hunter where it is by freezing in place. Retrievers get it after it has been brought down by the hunter. Setters locate the game by freezing ("setting") near it. And Spaniels "flush" or "spring" the game from its hiding place by rushing up to it.

Many of the breeds in this group are able to perform several of these jobs. Sporting dogs have an excellent ability to locate by smell, and many are able to carry things gently in their mouths. Sporting dogs like to be around people and interact with them. They need company. They've always worked side by side with people, so they pay attention and are quick learners. They are active and alert, so they need a good daily workout of play and exercise.

The Sporting breeds are:

American Water Spaniel	**German Wirehaired Pointer**
Brittany	**Golden Retriever**
Chesapeake Bay Retriever	**Gordon Setter**
Clumber Spaniel	**Irish Setter**
Cocker Spaniel	**Irish Water Spaniel**
Curly-Coated Retriever	**Labrador Retriever**
English Cocker Spaniel	**Pointer**
English Setter	**Sussex Spaniel**
English Springer Spaniel	**Vizsla**
Field Spaniel	**Weimaraner**
Flat-Coated Retriever	**Welsh Springer Spaniel**
German Shorthaired Pointer	**Wirehaired Pointing Griffon**

American Water Spaniel

This family-loving sporting dog has a long history of being among the most skillful of all hunters' companions: He can just as easily retrieve a downed quail from the thicket as he can swim like a seal to bring in a duck, using his rudder-like tail. Families will find him adaptable to both city and country living, but his life is not complete without some time splashing in the water.

The American Water Spaniel's history is not as well known as that of other sporting breeds, but it's generally believed that he descended from the old English Water Spaniel (now extinct), the Irish Water Spaniel, and the Curly-Coated Retriever. The latter two share his most unusual feature: a coat of dark brown, shiny curls or waves. He also has an undercoat to keep him warm in cold weather.

His face is smooth, and he does not have the fluff of curls on the top of his head that an Irish Water Spaniel does. His eyes can be the same color as his coat or lighter brown, although they shouldn't be bright lemon yellow. Unlike most spaniels' tails, his is not docked. It is covered with long, feathery hair. He needs this long tail to steer him around in the water, which is one reason he's such a good swimmer.

FUN FACTS

Like the Chesapeake Bay Retriever, the American Water Spaniel is one of the few breeds developed in the United States. He is the state dog of Wisconsin and can usually be found in the northern states of the Midwest: Wisconsin, Michigan, and Minnesota.

EXCERPTS FROM THE STANDARD

General Appearance:
An active, muscular dog, medium in size, with a wavy or curly brown coat. Intelligent, eager, yet controllable. Solidly built, full of strength and dignity.

Size, Proportion, and Substance:
Height—male or female, 15 to 18 inches.
Weight—males, 30 to 45 pounds; females, 25 to 40 pounds.
Slightly longer than tall.

USA

Sporting Dogs 41

The Brittany is a happy, alert, and active dog. He loves to work and is eager to please. With his medium size, beautiful orange- or liver-and-white coat, and soft expression, he is an appealing dog. He thrives on challenges and exercise, work and friendship, and makes an ideal dog for someone who can give him a serious daily workout.

Brittanys are hunting dogs; they point to birds hidden in forest brush or fields and then retrieve downed game. They get their name from their place of origin: the northern area of France called Brittany. Though lighter and taller, they look similar to Welsh Springer Spaniels. They may share the same ancestors. Brittany and Wales traded goods historically, and dogs could also have been exchanged or imported. In fact, Brittanys used to be called Brittany Spaniels, but in 1982, Spaniel was dropped from their name.

Brittanys need brushing or combing every few days and a scissors trim every few months.

EXCERPTS FROM THE STANDARD

General Appearance:
A compact dog of medium size, with legs long enough to allow agile, broad ground coverage. Strong, vigorous, energetic, and quick-moving. Rugged without being clumsy.

Size, Proportion, and Substance:
Height—17½ to 20½ inches at withers. Weight—between 30 and 40 pounds. Proportion—height equals length of body. Substance—not too delicate in bone, yet never heavy-boned or cumbersome.

FUN FACTS

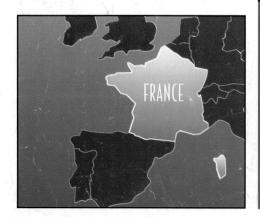
FRANCE

In the eighteenth and nineteenth centuries, wealthy landowners in Europe had huge forests filled with game birds and animals to hunt for fun. Meanwhile, their farm workers would sometimes hunt secretly at night with the help of their trusted dogs. This "poaching" or stealing of game, was illegal. If caught, poachers were punished severely by the local judges—often the very owners of the estates where the birds or rabbits were poached. Brittanys were considered excellent poaching dogs because they were obedient and quick as lightning in their work.

Chesapeake Bay Retriever

The Chesapeake Bay Retriever is a truly American breed, one whose birth took place quite by accident. In 1807 two Newfoundland puppies, one black, the other reddish brown, were rescued from a shipwreck off the coast of Maryland. They were bred to local mixed-breed retriever dogs, and probably later to Flat-Coated and Curly-Coated Retrievers, producing the "Chessie" type that appeared around 1884.

The Chesapeake has always had a cheery disposition but a seriousness of purpose toward his work. He faces the winter harshness with courage and an eagerness to perform his retrieving duties. He is a bold, strong, active dog, so he needs plenty of exercise every day. He especially likes swimming, so retrieving games are ideal throughout the summer and fall.

He has a fine, woolly undercoat for extra warmth. His coat resists water like a duck's feathers—when he leaves the water and shakes himself, his coat should be almost dry. Colors range from dark brown to tan to straw colored. A white spot on the chest, belly, or toes is allowed, but solid colors are preferred.

Feet are webbed; eyes are clear and pale, yellow to amber. The body displays power: His head is broad, his chest is deep, and his hindquarters are sometimes slightly higher than the shoulders.

EXCERPTS FROM THE STANDARD

General Appearance:
A bright and happy demeanor and an intelligent expression and impressive outlines, denoting a good worker. Courageous, alert, with a love of water and a solid disposition.

Size, Proportion, and Substance:
Height—males, 23 to 26 inches; females, 21 to 24. Weight—males, 65 to 80 pounds; females, 55 to 70.

USA

FUN FACTS

By the late nineteenth century, the Chesapeake type had definitely developed, though it was not exactly the dog we know today. At that time, hunters wanting to sell ducks as food to markets would shoot guns over the Chesapeake Bay, day and night. The dogs were expected to retrieve as many as 100 to 200 ducks per hunt. They were strong, sturdy dogs with thick, dark brown coats who braved the rough and icy waters of the Chesapeake Bay, as is still true, but all had longer, thicker coats than those sported by today's dogs.

Clumber Spaniel

The Clumber takes his time; he is a calm and friendly companion. Being low to the ground, the Clumber makes good use of his excellent smelling ability on walks, and he retrieves happily from the water. He likes to be with people and loves children.

The Clumber has a royal history. On the eve of the French Revolution, a French duke, the Duc de Noailles, managed to get his beloved spaniels out of the country to sanctuary in England. There they were taken in by an English nobleman, the Duke of Newcastle. He had a vast estate, located in Sherwood Forest, called Clumber Park. This is how the dog got its name.

Though the sweet-natured Clumber would love to be a lap dog, he's a little too heavy. His shape is somewhat like that of a Basset Hound, but he is bigger and has a longer coat. The coat is mostly white, with lemon or orange spots and freckles, and needs brushing only once or twice a week—but it does shed. The eyes are dark amber in color, with a gentle, soft expression.

FUN FACTS

Clumbers are one of the oldest spaniels. First developed in France, they are believed to be a mixture of Bassett Hound (the long, low body) and Alpine Spaniel (the heavy head). The Clumber Spaniel was one of the first 10 breeds recognized by the AKC; now he is one of the AKC's 10 rarest breeds.

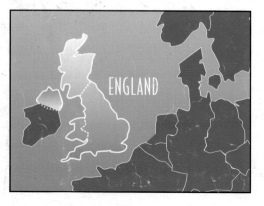

ENGLAND

EXCERPTS FROM THE STANDARD

General Appearance:
Heavy brow, deep chest, straight forelegs, and good feet show his power and endurance. Dignified, but having enthusiasm for work and play.

Size, Proportion, and Substance:
Height—males, about 19 to 20 inches at the withers; females, about 17 to 19 inches. Weight—males 70 to 80 pounds; females, 55 to 70 pounds.

Cocker Spaniel

With big baby eyes, soft coat, cozy size, and an upbeat personality, it's easy to see why the Cocker Spaniel is one of the most popular dogs in America. Cockers are sensitive and playful dogs, and they love people, often more than other dogs. He forms a tight, lifelong bond with his owner. The Cocker can adapt easily to city or country living, as long as he gets his exercise and playtime.

It may be hard to imagine now, but this little house dog was a highly respected hunter not so long ago. His game was the woodcock, a migratory European bird that the breed loved to dive after into the thick undergrowth and chase into the air. So it became known as the woodcock, or "Cocker," Spaniel.

The Cocker Spaniel has a beautiful, silky coat that is straight or wavy, but it doesn't get that way by itself. Daily brushing and professional grooming every three months are essential to the well-being of this dog. In dog shows, Cockers are judged in separate varieties by their colors: Black (can have some tan points); Any Solid Color Other than Black (ASCOB); solid colored with tan markings (a little bit of white on chest or throat is allowed); Parti-Color (mostly white with another color).

EXCERPTS FROM THE STANDARD

General Appearance:
The smallest of the sporting dogs, he is sturdy, speedy, and merry. His expression should be intelligent, alert, and soft. His tail is docked, and his step is sporty.

Size, Proportion, and Substance:
Height—males, 15 inches at the withers; females, 14 inches.

ENGLAND

FUN FACTS

Most Cockers are happy house pets. Some, however, have lived unusual lives. One Cocker, Chota Peg, lived at sea for 13 years as the dog of the skipper of the *SS United States*. She travelled a total of two million miles of ocean. Sergeant Boade, another Cocker Spaniel, parachuted 16 times with his owner, a military paratrooper.

The Curly-Coated Retriever, probably one of the oldest retriever breeds, is not simply a Labrador with curly hair. He is a distinct breed with his own personality—sensitive, intelligent, curious, and family-loving. Like all the retrievers, he loves his daily exercise, especially running and swimming.

His ancestors include the old English Water Spaniel (now extinct) and some form of retrieving setter. Also in his bloodlines is the Poodle, added around the late 1800s to strengthen his retrieving ability and tighten the curl in his coat.

His small, woolly curls cover his body, tail, and ears, and set him apart from other retrievers. It is a self-styling coat; a quick brushing twice a week is all it needs. Like the Chesapeake, the Curly can shake himself practically dry after leaving the water. That woolly coat helps keep out burrs and prickles, which makes Curlies fearless about going headfirst into any undergrowth. The Curly's coat can be black or liver; his eyes should not be yellow. His nails need frequent trimming and filing.

FUN FACTS

While most dogs mature at around two years old, the Curly behaves like an energetic puppy longer. He may settle down as late as four years old, though he's a puppy heart forever. The patient person with a sense of humor does best with the unique and gentle Curly-Coated Retriever.

ENGLAND

EXCERPTS FROM THE STANDARD

General Appearance:
A strong, rugged dog, showing activity, endurance, and intelligence. Body rather short and muscular; powerful legs.

Size, Proportion, and Substance:
Size and weight can vary from 21 to 30 inches and 50 to 100 pounds, though most are in the middle range. There are no size or weight requirements, quality of the dog being more important.

English Cocker Spaniel

EXCERPTS FROM THE STANDARD

General Appearance:
An active, merry sporting dog, compactly built. Alive with energy, powerful and ready to dive into dense brush to flush and retrieve game. Very active docked tail.

Size, Proportion, and Substance:
Height at withers—males, 16 to 17 inches; females, 15 to 16 inches. Weight—males, 28 to 34 pounds; females 26 to 32 pounds. Height slightly greater than length.

ENGLAND

The English Cocker Spaniel was considered merely a variety of Cocker Spaniel until 1935, when the English Cocker Spaniel Club of America was founded. Spaniels were first differentiated by size—the larger ones springing game and the smaller ones hunting woodcock. These types became the Springers and Cockers. Dog people in this country refined the Cocker even more to create the Cocker Spaniel, while the English Cocker stayed truer to the original Cocker.

Like the American, the English Cocker Spaniel is sensitive. Handled with tenderness and respect, he makes a willing learner. English Cockers are joyful, entertaining, and active friends to all people.

English Cockers' coats have the same sorts of colors and markings as American: solid black, liver, or red; parti-color (white with color markings); and tan markings with solid colors. Their eyes have a soft, loving expression, and should be dark brown or hazel in the liver Cockers. The tail is docked. Like the Cocker's, the English Cocker's coat requires a commitment to regular grooming.

FUN FACTS

The English poet Elizabeth Barrett Browning had a Cocker in the 1840s named Flush. Her devotion to her dog—and his to her—is recorded in her letters: "He will sleep at nights, now, nowhere except with his head on my shoulder. . . . If you were but to see him eat partridge from a silver fork. . . . Of course, he has given up his ice creams for the season, and the favorite substitute seems to be coffee . . . not poured into the saucer, but taken out of my little coffee cup." She even wrote a poem about him called "Flush or Faunus."

English Setter

The English Setter is an active, rugged dog, but also sweet and mild-mannered. He is happy being a true member of the family and likes to go on family outings. He makes a devoted companion.

The English Setter was developed in England, of course, where the breed goes back more than 400 years. One ancestor was the Spanish Pointer, who gave him his hunting abilities. Others include the large Water and Springer Spaniels, who gave him his long coat and docile temperament.

All English Setters are long and graceful, but also sturdy and muscular. The coat requires twice-weekly grooming. It is silky and flat, with a white background. The markings are tricolor, liver, blue, lemon or orange "belton" (salt and pepper sprinklings). Eyes and nose should be dark.

EXCERPTS FROM THE STANDARD

General Appearance:
Elegant, substantial, and symmetrical in build. Flat-coated with feathering of good length.

Size, Proportion, and Substance:
Height—males, about 25 inches; females, about 24 inches.

FUN FACTS

The English Setter, like all setters, works with the hunter to find the game, point, and then quickly "set" near the game. Before guns, hunters would throw out a large net to cover the area of tall grass or brush where the birds were hiding, then collect them. The setters stayed still while this happened.

ENGLAND

English Spring Spaniel

ENGLAND

The English Springer Spaniel is a medium-size, fun-loving dog adaptable to city or country life. He has the typical spaniel personality: smart, adoring, and eager to please. These dogs thrive on exercise and training. Springers learn quickly and remember well.

English Springer Spaniels are used for hunting and field trials (competitions of hunting skills), and are also show dogs or family companions. Springers are prized for their eagerness and ability to find and scare up a large variety of game birds as well as rabbits. In the field, they are light, lean, and fast. In the showring, their coats are longer and their expression may be softer. He is every inch a sporting dog of combined beauty and utility.

Springer Spaniel colors are primarily liver and white or black and white; some have those colors with tan points on eyebrows, cheeks, inside of ears, and under the tail.

FUN FACTS

The word *Springer* in this dog's name comes from the job he does as a hunter. Originally considered just a spaniel, his larger size made him better able to "spring" game in thickets and underbrush. His shorter siblings hunted woodcocks, and thus Springer Spaniels and Cocker Spaniels began to be bred separately.

Field Spaniels came about as a breed in the late 1800s when Welsh Cockers were crossed with Sussex Spaniels and English Water Spaniels, creating a long, low spaniel. Later Springer and Cocker lines were introduced to achieve a more balanced, substantial dog to suit his purpose as a hunter's companion.

Eager and hardworking, with a good scenting ability, the Field Spaniel is an enthusiastic retriever with great endurance and noble attitude. He is an active and energetic dog who can live anywhere as long as he gets lots of daily exercise.

He has sturdy legs and big feet with soft hair between the toes (that needs occasional trimming). His dense, glossy coat, wavy and feathery, is usually black or liver, but can also be golden liver, or roan (different colors of single hairs) and have tan markings. His tail is docked, to balance his overall appearance.

FUN FACTS

The obedient, fun-loving Field Spaniel is one of the least-known spaniels. That is because of the great popularity of his cousins, the English Springer and the Cocker Spaniels. Actually, the breed almost died out in the 1950s. All of today's Field Spaniels are directly descended from four dogs.

ENGLAND

EXCERPTS FROM THE STANDARD

General Appearance:
A substantial hunter and companion of medium size, active and strong, solid and muscular; both noble and affectionate; sometimes reserved with strangers.

Size, Proportion, and Substance:
Height—males, ideal size 18 inches; females, ideal size 17 inches at withers.

Flat-Coated Retriever

The Flat-Coated Retriever combines gracefulness in looks with grace of character. This is a loving, playful dog that needs a strong personal relationship with his owner and daily exercise. Most are so good-natured that they would rather make friends than anything else. He is intelligent and adapts well to changes around him.

The Flat-Coated Retriever developed as a variety of the English retriever type that existed in the early 1800s. The large Newfoundland was bred with the setter, sheepdog, and spaniel-like water dogs.

Though sturdy and solid, the Flat-Coated Retriever has a sleek silhouette. His head is less boxy than those of other retrievers. His brow is high; his expression is lively. His solid black or liver coat is thick and glossy and lies flat, although sometimes it may be slightly wavy. He moves with grace and flowing ease.

FUN FACTS

Despite the Flat-Coated Retriever's engaging personality, in the early 1900s Labradors and Golden Retrievers overshadowed the Flat-Coat in popularity. The breed began to dwindle to small numbers, but by the mid-1960s the Flat-Coated Retriever was again more frequently found. He is still fairly rare in the United States.

EXCERPTS FROM THE STANDARD

General Appearance:
The Flat-Coated Retriever is a versatile family companion and hunting retriever with a happy and active demeanor, intelligent expression, and clean lines. He is powerful without clumsiness, and lively but not nervous.

Size, Proportion, and Substance:
Height—males, 23 to 24 1/2 inches at the withers; females, 22 to 23 1/2 inches. Length is slightly more than height.

ENGLAND

German Shorthaired Pointer

The German Shorthaired Pointer is a medium-size, versatile sporting dog. He is also an even-tempered and loyal family watchdog and companion. His endurance, intelligence, and nobility are reflected in his handsome appearance: a deep chest, smooth pace, and dignified expression.

The German Shorthaired Pointer was carefully developed in Germany over the late 1800s to produce the multitalented dog of today. Many dogs were mixed together to create one dog with many skills. It began with the crossing of some kind of German bird dog with the old Spanish Pointer, a heavy and somewhat slow dog with an excellent scenting ability. Local scenting hounds, as well as English Foxhounds, were bred into the dogs to add tracking skills and duck hunting over water to the dog's traits. English Pointers were brought into the breeding process to add quickness, grace, and their elegant, highly held nose.

All German Shorthaired Pointers are solid liver or liver and white; no other colors are allowed. A quick weekly brushing is all their coats need. Their gentle, good-humored eyes should be brown, the darker the better. The tail is docked to less than half its original length.

EXCERPTS FROM THE STANDARD

General Appearance:
Noble and well-balanced; his form reflects power, endurance, agility, intelligence, and energy. He shows keen enthusiasm for his work and is not nervous or flighty.

Size, Proportion, and Substance:
Height—males, 23 to 25 inches at withers; females, 21 to 23 inches. Weight—males, 55 to 70 pounds; females, 45 to 60 pounds.

FUN FACTS

This is a great dog for a family that likes outdoor activities. The German Shorthaired Pointer is strong willed, so obedience training is a good idea. He is affectionate with his family.

GERMANY

German Wirehaired Pointer

The German Wirehaired Pointer shares many qualities of the German Shorthaired Pointer, while still having his own definite identity. In England, hunters wanted their dogs to specialize in certain sports, but the Germans wanted an all-around hunting dog that could find game, point, and retrieve. There was a general group of German wirehaired dogs with differing ancestors, and they were allowed to interbreed. The eventual result, the German Wirehaired Pointer, reflects traits drawn originally from the English Pointer, the Foxhound, the German Shorthaired Pointer, and the hunting Poodle. He is good on scenting, with a tough constitution, and the coat—and courage—to face and encounter any terrain.

His color is solid liver or liver and white, with no black allowed. Tails are docked to less than half of their original length. Feet are webbed for swimming and have thick pads for covering rough terrain.

FUN FACTS

The German Wirehaired Pointer's coat sets him apart from the German Shorthaired Pointer. A perfect all-weather covering, it consists of an outer coat that is straight, harsh, and wiry. It lies flat and is largely water repellent, for protection while water retrieving. It also protects his skin from the harsh brush and briars so he can go into any kind of terrain. Extra protection comes from the heavy growth of hair around his face. He has bushy eyebrows and a short beard and whiskers. The coat is shorter on the top of his head, and extra thick on his shoulders and at the base of his tail.

GERMANY

Golden Retriever

Golden Retrievers are serious about their retrieving work, but they have just as much fun being silly. They like everybody. They are kids at heart and may take a little longer than some other dogs to settle into adult behavior. However, their great physical strength combined with their eagerness to please make them highly trainable.

The Golden was developed in Scotland, beginning with the crossing of a yellow English retriever and a rugged water spaniel. The smaller Newfoundland retrieving dog, Irish Setters, other water spaniels, and possibly a Bloodhound were added at various times. The dog has developed an excellent nose.

Goldens have thick and lustrous coats that range in color from deep to light honey gold. The Golden's lighter puppy coat deepens to its true color after about a year. It can be straight or wavy and needs brushing twice a week. The eyes are dark brown, and the tail is a lively plume that floats straight out or curls up slightly.

ENGLAND

FUN FACTS

Goldens are easy to train and strong, but their most outstanding trait is character. They are outgoing and devoted companions to all sorts of people, happy, and trusting. But they can also be protective. One infant's life was saved when her neighbor's Golden held the baby by the edge of her dress. The dog kept the baby from falling off a deck with a 50-foot drop until the dog's owners came to help.

EXCERPTS FROM THE STANDARD

General Appearance:
A symmetrical, powerful, active dog, sound, and well put together, not clumsy or long in the leg, displaying a kindly expression and possessing a personality that is eager, alert, and self-confident.

Size, Proportion, and Substance:
Height—males, 23 to 24 inches at withers; females, 21 1/2 to 22 1/2 inches. Length slightly greater than height. Weight—males, 65 to 75 pounds; females, 55 to 65 pounds.

Gordon Setter

Among the three types of setters, the Gordon represents the Scottish side of the family and is the largest and heaviest of them. Gordons are muscular, big-boned, and sturdy. They are highly intelligent, quick to train, and have good memories. The breed has been around since the 1600s or earlier. Like other setters, it developed from the Spanish Pointer and early spaniels. In the 1700s, the fourth Duke of Gordon became the first person to concentrate on breeding a distinct Scottish setter.

Gordons thrive on plenty of vigorous exercise and interaction with their owners, and mature at about four years of age. Today's Gordons have lustrous, black feathery coats. Their markings are a deep mahogany color: a small spot over each eye, on the sides of the muzzle, on the throat and chest, inside and around the hind legs, and at the bottom of the front legs.

EXCERPTS FROM THE STANDARD

General Appearance:
Active, upstanding, and stylish, with a strong, rather short back. Head is fairly heavy and finely formed. His movements are smooth-flowing.

Size, Proportion, and Substance:
Height—males, 24 to 27 inches; females, 23 to 26 inches. Weight—males, 55 to 80 pounds; females, 45 to 70 pounds.
The length is about equal to the height.

SCOTLAND

FUN FACTS

This breed is named after the fourth Duke's Gordon Castle Kennels and the sixth Duke of Gordon, whose setters in the early 1800s became the model for today's dog. The breed's motto is "beauty, brains, and bird sense."

Irish Setter

The Irish Setter is known for his glossy, long, red coat and graceful movements. He is valued even more for his lively playfulness and carefree sweetness.

The Irish Setter is a likable dog: friendly, loving, loyal, and protective. He enjoys the company of children. In fact, he takes a while to grow up himself. He's usually about three years old before he settles into adulthood.

He likes plenty of room to run, vigorous exercise, and loving attention. He is curious and people-oriented. In fact, sometimes field trial competitors complain that the dog is more interested in playing with his handler than he is in trying to win prizes.

Though the breed was developed in the early 1700s in Ireland, the exact origins are unknown. Most likely, the Irish Setter came from an English or Gordon Setter, spaniel, and pointer combination.

EXCERPTS FROM THE STANDARD

General Appearance:
An active, aristocratic dog, rich red in color, substantial yet elegant. More than two feet tall at the withers, with a straight, fine, glossy coat. A sweet-natured, trainable companion.

Size, Proportion, and Substance:
There is no disqualification as to size; balance and fitness are more important. The ideal, however, is, for males, 27 inches at the withers and about 70 pounds, and for females, 25 inches tall and 60 pounds. The body is slightly longer than it is tall.

FUN FACTS

The Irish Setter is slimmer than the English or Gordon Setters. His head is longer, and his red coat is straighter. He is one of the largest of the sporting breeds.

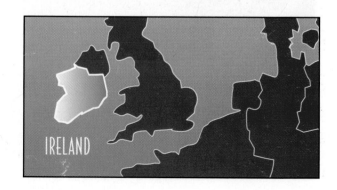
IRELAND

Irish Water Spaniel

The big, bold Irish Water Spaniel has an ancient history. Archaeologists have found remains of an Irish Water Spaniel–type dog dating all the way back to the seventh or eighth century.

IRELAND

The tallest of all spaniels, Irish Water Spaniels are alert and curious. They combine great intelligence with a dashing, ready-to-go attitude that speaks of their history as hardworking water dogs.

The Irish Water Spaniel loves people and becomes deeply attached to his family. He is cautious around strangers. Because of his size and devotion to the family, he makes an impressive watchdog.

The Irish Water Spaniel may resemble a Poodle, but his looks are definitely his own. First is the floppy "topknot" of loose curls that crowns his head, and second is his "rat tail," thick at the base with some curl, and then smoothly tapering to a fine point at the end. His liver-colored coat must be cared for on a regular schedule, two to four times a week.

EXCERPTS FROM THE STANDARD

General Appearance:
Smart, proud, strong sporting dog; great intelligence combined with rugged endurance and a bold, dashing eagerness in personality.

Size, Proportion, and Substance:
Height—males, 22 to 24 inches at the withers; females, 21 to 23 inches. Weight—males 55 to 65 pounds; females 45 to 58 pounds

FUN FACTS

Irish Water Spaniels are used more for retrieving ducks than for chasing out birds, as most spaniels do. That's because Irish Water Spaniels have sharp retrieving skills and love the water. Their tightly curled coats are oily and naturally water-resistant. In AKC hunting tests and field trials, they are considered retrievers.

Labrador Retriever

The beloved Labrador Retriever is playful, loving to people and hardworking. The Lab can be counted on as a true friend anytime, anyplace, and is highly respected for his prowess at many jobs: as a guide for the disabled, a search-and-rescue dog, and for narcotics detection.

Labs originated from the original "St. John's" water dogs of Newfoundland—rugged dogs who worked alongside the fishermen of Newfoundland, helping them pull in nets and even catching fish that escaped from fishing lines. Over the years, Labs developed into the retrievers we know today when they were crossed with setters, spaniels, and other retrievers.

Labs used to be best known for their glossy black coats, but yellow and chocolate Labs are growing in numbers. Any of the Labs can have a small white spot on the chest, but all should have dark (not pink) noses. The coat is short and dense and sheds year-round. Eyes range from yellow to hazel to brown or black.

LABRADOR

EXCERPTS FROM THE STANDARD

General Appearance:
Strongly built, very active, muscular in the hindquarters. Tail should not curl over the back.

Size, Proportion, and Substance:
Height at withers—males, 22 ½ to 24 ½ inches; females, 21 ½ to 23 ½ inches. Weight—males, 60 to 75 pounds; females, 55 to 70 pounds.

FUN FACTS

The Lab has a distinctive tail. It is covered with thick, short (not feathery) hair. It is wide at the base and tapers to a point. It should not curl over the back. It is called an "otter" tail because of its rounded shape.

Pointer

The Pointer knows how to do his job, and he takes pride in doing it well. His short, smooth coat shows off his handsome outline. He is sleek, muscular, and ready for action. The Pointer is an independent dog who likes to compete. His concentration is intense. He has strength, courage, and great dignity, but he is also a sweet companion and gentle with children.

The Pointer follows the scent of prey and then comes to a completely frozen position close to it, often raising up a front leg. This is called pointing. After the dog freezes into the point, he stays there until released by the handler. Working to locate birds in the field is his heart's greatest desire.

Records exist for the Pointer in England as far back as 1650. The Pointer is most likely made up of Foxhound, Greyhound, and Bloodhound, plus some early "setting spaniel."

A Pointer's eyes should be dark. His tail tapers to a fine point, and never curls up over his back. One distinctive feature of the Pointer is his upraised nose: When pointing or posing, he shows himself as true sporting royalty.

FUN FACTS

In the early 1700s the English Pointer was bred with the Spanish Pointer to improve the dog's pointing ability even more. The pointing urge is so strong in this breed that puppies only a few months old may start pointing without any instruction or training.

ENGLAND

EXCERPTS FROM THE STANDARD

General Appearance:
Expressing compact power and agile grace; the head is noble and proud; intelligent and alert; muscular, showing both endurance and dash. A wide-awake, hard-driving hunting dog with stamina, courage, and the desire to go.

Size, Proportion, and Substance:
Balance and symmetry are more important in the Pointer than size. However, size falls within a range. Height for males, 25 to 28 inches; females, 23 to 26 inches. Weight for males, 55 to 75 pounds; females, 45 to 65 pounds.

Sussex Spaniel

ENGLAND

EXCERPTS FROM THE STANDARD

General Appearance:
Long and low, rectangular and muscular in appearance, but freely moving and serious.

Size, Proportion, and Substance:
Height—13 to 15 inches. Weight—35 to 45 pounds. Longer in body than tall.

Though small in size, the Sussex is one of the most dignified of spaniels. He has a serious but soft and contented expression. He moves slowly and deliberately, with a gently rolling gait, his head held low. Like all spaniels, he enjoys the close companionship of his family. He loves them dearly, and is especially fond of children.

The Sussex gets his name from his place of origin, the county of Sussex in southern England. There he was bred as a hunting dog, to drive out game from underbrush into the hunters' view, and then to retrieve it for them. His keen nose makes up for his pace, which is slower than the Cocker's and Springer's.

The Sussex has the long, low, and heavy look of the Clumber Spaniel, though the Sussex is smaller. He has short legs and a thick body. His head is also heavy, with an overhanging brow and long feathery ears that are covered with soft, wavy hair. His lustrous coat is one of his most beautiful features—thick and wavy, in a rich golden liver color. The tail is docked.

Vizsla

Bright as a newly shined copper penny, the sleek, gentle Vizsla is the national hunting dog of Hungary. The name is pronounced VEESH-la, and the word *vizsla* means "obedient and alert" in Hungarian.

The breed was developed among the wandering tribes in central Hungary hundreds of years ago, and has remained true to its early form. In outline the Vizsla resembles the German Shorthaired Pointer, but he is smaller and more delicate. Art dating back to the tenth century shows a hunter with a dog resembling the Vizsla. The dog was valued as a scenter, pointer, and retriever.

Vizslas have energy galore. Their owners will have fun keeping them busy. Vizslas are fun to train because they are eager to prove how much they love their owners. They are smart and learn quickly. They are also sensitive, so gentle corrections go a long way.

EXCERPTS FROM THE STANDARD

General Appearance:
A medium-sized, short-coated hunting dog of distinguished appearance. Lightly built but powerful.

Size, Proportion, and Substance:
Height—males, 22 to 24 inches at withers; females, 21 to 23 inches.

FUN FACTS

The Vizsla was developed in gentle, farming lands. Because his glossy coat has only one layer, with no undercoat, he is not designed to withstand cold climates. The Hungarians call his coat color *sarga*, which means "bread-crust." And that lovely, warm color should also be seen on his nose, eyes, and even inside his mouth.

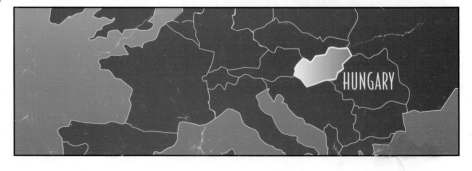

HUNGARY

Weimaraner

The Weimaraner is a big, bold dog. His name is pronounced WY-mah-rah-ner or VY-mah-rah-ner, a word that comes from the German republic of Weimar, where this fairly recent breed was born in the early 1800s. They were hunting dogs bred strictly by and for aristocrats, and are believed to be descended from Bloodhounds and Red Schweisshunds, though the Weimaraner is larger than those breeds. They were first used to hunt game such as wolves, mountain lions, and bears, though now birds are their main prey.

Weimaraners are smart, and their busy minds thrive on activity. They are strong and determined, needing time, space, and attention. If you want the challenges of keeping ahead of the fearless "gray ghost," and your daily activities can include your dog, you may be suited to the Weimaraner. He loves kids and is used to being a member of a family.

His silvery coat, sometimes called "mouse grey," should be solid colored; a small white spot on the chest is allowed. Eyes range from light amber to gray to blue-gray and should express his intelligence and good humor. The nose is gray, and the tail is docked to six inches.

While the artist William Wegman was trying to take photographs in his studio, his Weimaraner puppy kept getting underfoot. So Wegman put the puppy, Man Ray, to work as a model. Throughout the 1970s, Man Ray's striking beauty, hammy poses, and air of self-confidence made for powerful pictures. Fay Ray began working in the mid-1980s. Now her daughter, Battina, has joined the fun.

EXCERPTS FROM THE STANDARD

General Appearance:
A picture of grace, nobility, speed, stamina, and alertness.

Size, Proportion, and Substance:
Height—males, 25 to 27 inches; females, 23 to 25 inches at the withers.

GERMANY

Welsh Springer Spaniel

As the name says, the Welsh Springer Spaniel comes from Wales originally, and that is where most of them can be found today. Welshies are descended from among the oldest hunting dogs, and date back as early as 250 B.C., when their native land was occupied by wild Celtic or Gallic tribes.

The Welsh Springer Spaniel is an eager and quick learner, extremely affectionate, and devoted. The Welshie's lovely red-and-white coat is straight and soft, not wavy or curly, and requires moderate upkeep. Regular brushing will do the job. The coat is dense—its heritage from centuries of retrieving—to protect it from the water. It sheds twice a year. The Welshie has gentle brown eyes, a black or brown nose, and a docked tail.

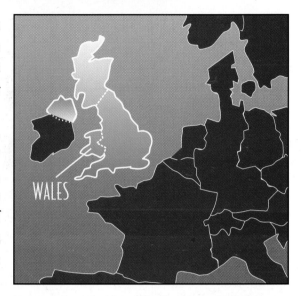

WALES

EXCERPTS FROM THE STANDARD

General Appearance:
A distinct dog of ancient origin; compact, not leggy, and hardworking.

Size, Proportion, and Substance:
Height—males, 18 to 19 inches at the withers; females, 17 to 18 inches. The length of the body may be slightly longer or the same as the height, but not less.

The Welsh Springer Spaniel is smaller than the English Springer, but stronger than the Cocker Spaniel. He has shorter legs and a longer coat than the Brittany, with a larger head and longer ears. All Welshies are distinguished by their beautiful coats—always red with white.

Wirehaired Pointing Griffon

EXCERPTS FROM THE STANDARD

General Appearance:
Medium-sized, with a noble, square-shaped head; strong, able to cover all kinds of terrain. Moves gracefully.

Size, Proportion, and Substance:
Height—males, 22 to 24 inches; females, 20 to 22 inches at the withers. Slightly longer than tall.

These dogs are called "griffons" because of their wiry coats and the extra hair on their faces. In ancient myths, a griffon was a fierce creature that was half lion and half eagle. But this Griffon isn't fierce. Most people today find these shaggy faces lovable and even sweetly comical.

The Wirehaired Pointing Griffon is a gentle and intelligent whiskered dog. The quiet country life is what this dog loves best. He blossoms in a steady, low-key—but high exercise—family. Long, long runs through fields and then some time in the water with his favorite person are his idea of heaven. He is a sensitive dog who pays attention and will respond quickly to a gentle trainer.

Although the breed was established in the late 1800s by a wealthy Dutchman, it was developed mostly in France. The dog was bred to be a slow, careful hunter with a good nose and fine pointing and retrieving skills.

The Wirehaired Pointing Griffon's most distinguishing characteristic is his coat. It is usually brown and gray, of medium length and straight, never curly or woolly. The harshness of it protects the dog from briars, bushes, and the cold. He has a large moustache and big, bushy eyebrows.

HOUNDS

There are two kinds of Hounds: scent hounds and sighthounds. Scent hounds hunt with their noses, sighthounds with their eyes. Both are some of the oldest kinds of dogs used by man to help him hunt.

Hounds tend to work independently. They move ahead of the hunter to track down and corner the prey. Many have a "baying" bark or song, while others have a sharp bark. These sounds let the hunter know where they are once they've found the prey.

Hounds are sweet and loving with people, but sometimes their "ears turn off when their noses turn on," as a popular scent hound-owner saying goes. Tracking an intriguing smell is what the scent hounds love to do most, even if you're in a hurry to do something else. The sighthounds are agile and fast, so be sure to keep them on a lead when you're not in a safely enclosed area with them. Overall, hounds are good-natured and want to please you.

The scent hounds are:

Basset Hound

Beagle

Black and Tan Coonhound

Bloodhound

Dachshund

Foxhound, American

Foxhound, English

Harrier

Otterhound

Petit Basset Griffon Vendéen

The sighthounds are:

Afghan Hound

Basenji

Borzoi

Greyhound

Ibizan Hound

Irish Wolfhound

Norwegian Elkhound

Pharaoh Hound

Rhodesian Ridgeback

Saluki

Scottish Deerhound

Whippet

Afghan Hound

When there were kings in Afghanistan, they were sure to have a kennel of Afghan Hounds, a breed that has lived in that country for more years than we know. These dogs accompanied the royal hunting party, following the sight of their prey.

Afghan Hounds were used to hunt animals ranging from wolves, wild dogs, and snow leopards to mountain deer, antelope, and rabbits. The breed was introduced to Britain in the late 1800s.

Because their country of origin has both steep mountains and vast deserts, there is variety in the types of Afghans. Most of those that live in Western Europe, Britain, and the United States fit into one of two types: The "mountain" type tends to be darker, with a heavier coat; the "desert" type is longer and leaner, with a thinner and lighter-colored coat.

The Afghan's hunting instincts are still strong. If properly exercised with long daily walks and a good hard run as often as possible, he will be quiet and happy in the house. He is good with children when raised with them.

FUN FACTS

Afghan Hound owners must be prepared to spend lots of time grooming. Those luxurious coats require three to six hours of brushing every week. The Afghan puppy has a short coat, but by his third birthday the coat has grown to its full glory.

AFGHANISTAN

EXCERPTS FROM THE STANDARD

General Appearance:
An aristocrat, dignified and aloof. Carries his head proudly, gazing far off into the distance. Coat is long and silky with a long topknot.

Size, Proportion, and Substance:
Height—males about 27 inches; females, about 25 inches at the withers. Weight—males, about 60 pounds; females about 50 pounds.

Basenji

The name is pronounced Buh-SEN-jee, and they are best known for their bark: They haven't got one. They don't bark, but they do make sounds. When they are happy, they chortle or yodel softly, and they have a sad wail when they're unhappy. Usually, however, they're quiet.

But that doesn't mean they're still. Basenjis are busy and playful little dogs. They like lots of exercise and attention. Basenjis originated in central Africa and were presented to the pharaohs of ancient Egypt as gifts. Though the pharaohs eventually disappeared from history, the Basenji survived. They continued to be valued in Africa for their intelligence, speed, hunting ability, and silence. Wooden rattles or bells were sometimes put around the Basenji's neck so hunters could locate the dog. They are still used in Africa for pointing and retrieving as well as chasing their prey into nets.

In the late 1930s, Basenjis were brought to England and the United States, and the breed became established worldwide.

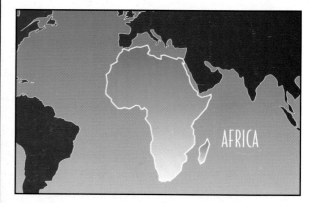

AFRICA

FUN FACTS

Even though he is strong and courageous in character, the Basenji also cares about being tidy in his appearance. His tail is curled up neatly into a circle on his rump. He has a short, glossy coat that he keeps sparkling clean by licking it as a cat does. His coat is usually a chestnut red color, with white socks, chest, and tip of tail. He can also be black and chestnut red, black, or brindle (black stripes), but always has the white markings. The coat only needs a once-a-week brushing. He has a foxy face, with wrinkles that sometimes give him a quizzical expression.

EXCERPTS FROM THE STANDARD

General Appearance:
Small, short-haired, and lightly built. Elegant and graceful, poised and curious, with a tightly curled tail.

Size, Proportion, and Substance:
Height—males, 17 inches; females, 16 inches. Weight—males, 24 pounds; females, 22 pounds.

Basset Hound

Long and low to the ground, the Basset Hound is renowned for his sweet personality and gentle manners.

The Basset is originally from France. He gets his name from the French word *bas*, which means "low." In the Middle Ages, French monks mixed a variety of hounds to produce a dog that could hunt low to the ground, following the scent of rabbits or deer over trails. This form of hunting was a popular sport for French aristocrats for hundreds of years.

As a hunter, the Basset can trail, flush, and even retrieve game. His sense of smell is second only to the Bloodhound's. And there's no mistaking when he has picked up the scent of his prey: He bays loudly and excitedly. He moves at a slow and steady pace, determined to get to that rabbit.

As a family companion, especially for kids, the Basset is a winner. He brings his easygoing, laid-back style into the house and is extremely devoted.

Bassets are usually black, brown, and white; those colors are acceptable in any combination or pattern. The coat is smooth and short, and a firm brushing once a week should keep it clean.

EXCERPTS FROM THE STANDARD

General Appearance:
Short-legged, heavy in bone, moving deliberately but not clumsily.

Size, Proportion, and Substance:
Height—preferably no higher than 14 inches at the withers; more than 15 inches is a disqualification.

FUN FACTS

There's something universally appealing about the Basset Hound's looks and character. Consequently, he's been a media star of sorts, being the mascot for Hush Puppy shoes and the star of the comic strip "Fred Basset," by A. Graham. A Basset named Quincy is a guest on the TV series *Coach*, and one named Cleo was the star of a 1960s TV series called *The People's Choice*.

FRANCE

Beagle

While cuteness may be your first impression of Beagles, these little dogs are actually part of a noble hound history. Hounds were used for scent hunting by the ancient Greeks. In the time of King Arthur, the Prince of Wales had his own special kind of hound, a white dog. And by the time of Queen Elizabeth I in the 1500s, most country gentlemen had packs of hounds.

The larger hounds tracked down deer, while the smaller ones went after rabbits. These were the first Beagles. Even today, there are Beagles that are trained in groups, or packs, to hunt rabbits. "Beagling" makes for an exciting afternoon outing.

Because Beagles lived in packs for so many hundreds of years, they just naturally like being together with people and other animals. They are gentle, happy companions, as loving as they are lovable. They are also clever, quick, and, most of all, curious. They need plenty of active exercise.

EXCERPTS FROM THE STANDARD

General Appearance:
Solid and sturdy, with a gentle, pleading expression. They can be any hound color, but are usually tan, black, and white.

Size, Proportion, and Substance:
There are two types of Beagles—those under 13 inches high (at the withers) and those over 13 inches high but no higher than 15 inches. Size is the only difference.

ENGLAND

FUN FACTS

The most famous Beagle, of course, is Snoopy. Charles Schulz got the idea for Snoopy from his own childhood dog, Spike. Soon Snoopy became a regular part of the "Peanuts" comic strip. Started in 1950, "Peanuts" is the most successful comic strip ever, and Snoopy is a big reason why.

Black and Tan Coonhound

The Black and Tan Coonhound looks something like his cousin the Bloodhound, from whom he's descended. But he is leaner and doesn't have the wrinkles in his face that the Bloodhound has. His outline is smooth. This dog was developed in the southern United States, and among his other ancestors are Foxhounds, including the Virginia Foxhound of Colonial days.

The Black and Tan Coonhound likes lots of fresh air and action-packed exercise. He loves to be with people, though he can be suspicious of strangers, and he may not take to new dogs right away. The Black and Tan, properly exercised, behaves nicely in the house (though he may expect to snuggle up on the sofa). He sheds year round, but weekly brushing keeps this under control.

The Black and Tan is serious when it comes to hunting. He is called "Coonhound" with good reason. When he picks up the scent of a raccoon and chases it up a tree, he bays loudly. This singing is called "barking up."

EXCERPTS FROM THE STANDARD

General Appearance:
A working hound, capable of withstanding harsh winters and hot summers with courage, friendliness, power, agility, and alertness.

Size, Proportion, and Substance:
Height—males, 25 to 27 inches at the withers; females, 23 to 25 inches.

FUN FACTS

A Black and Tan Coonhound inspired this famous tribute to dogs, written in the late nineteenth century by United States Senator George Vest of Missouri:

The one absolutely unselfish friend that man can have in this selfish world is his dog. He will kiss the hand that has no food to offer, he will lick the wounds and sores that come in encounters with the roughness of the world.

He guards the sleep of his pauper master as if he were a prince. When all other friends desert, he remains.

USA

Bloodhound

Part of the joy of owning a Bloodhound is training him to track a scent. You'll both have fun, and you might even be able to help your community should someone need to find a missing person!

The Bloodhounds' scenting ability is intense. All they really need is an article of clothing belonging to the missing person: They take a sniff and can follow the scent anywhere. In the 1100s, the most powerful people in Europe, including bishops, kept packs of Bloodhounds. Monasteries and aristocratic families took great care with their Bloodhounds' breeding. Some people believe that they got their name because of the care taken with the "blood lines," or family histories, of the dogs, and not because they follow the scent of blood on the trail.

The Bloodhound is a large dog and strong. His owner must be prepared to handle him with both respect and discipline. He is also one of the kindest and gentlest of all dogs. Bloodhounds are intelligent and want to please.

FUN FACTS

The wrinkly faced Bloodhound is often used to find people, including children, who have been lost for days or criminals on the run. The Bloodhound can follow a trail over a hundred miles to locate someone, even if he has to swim across water. And he can pick out the person he is tracking from a crowd. These dogs do not give up. When the Bloodhound finally finds what he's after, he does not attack the person he has been trailing. The Bloodhound is as sweet and affectionate as he is determined.

EXCERPTS FROM THE STANDARD

General Appearance:
Powerful, with thin, loose skin, especially around head and neck, where it hangs in loose folds. Possessing a wise and noble expression.

Size, Proportion, and Substance:
Height—males, 25 to 27 inches at the withers; females, 23 to 25 inches; for both, the greater height is preferred. Weight—males, 90 to 110 pounds preferred; females, 80 to 100 pounds preferred.

MEDITERRANEAN EUROPE

Borzoi

The Borzoi used to be known as the Russian Wolfhound, a breed named after his country and purpose: hunting wolves in the dense forests of his native Russia. He was bred for centuries by the Russian noble class to chase wolves in gigantic and elaborate hunts that often included hundreds of people and other breeds of dogs. After the Borzoi had caught the wolf, he was required to pin the animal down with his strong jaws until the arrival of the huntsmen, who usually freed the wolf back into the forest.

Borzois were imported to America in the 1890s, and have been appreciated here ever since for their gentle, dignified manner and their impressive abilities as swift lure coursers. Lure coursing is a sport in which a hound chases after a lure of three plastic bags speeding over a course, or track. It requires stamina, speed, and agility.

Borzois enjoy long runs and cold weather, but are quiet in the house.

EXCERPTS FROM THE STANDARD

General Appearance:
Elegant, a sound runner, with strong neck and jaws, graceful in motion or when still.

Size, Proportion, and Substance:
Height—males, at least 28 inches at withers; females, at least 26 inches. Weight—males, 75 to 105 pounds; females, 50 to 90 pounds.

FUN FACTS

Borzois are larger and heavier-coated than Greyhounds. Their long, silky coats can be straight, wavy, or curly. The hair on the face and fronts of legs is short. Borzois are usually white with another color such as lemon, tan, gray, or black. And they do shed. A daily brushing helps.

RUSSIA

Dachshund

The Dachshund has a lively, upbeat personality—spunky, curious, and friendly. These traits remain from the Dachshund's original job: "Dachshund" means "badger dog" in German, and he was created to hunt down badgers.

Badger dogs of some type have existed since the 1400s. The Dachshund as a specific breed has been around since the early 1600s. He is a digger so that he could dig his way into the badger's underground den. He is low and long so that he could fit inside the den to go after the badger. He is an eager hunter. He also loves to play and clown around. He is happy in the city or country, as long as he gets his daily exercise. Because of his long back, he shouldn't be allowed to jump from heights, including furniture.

Dachshunds can have one of three kinds (varieties) of coat: smooth, wirehaired, or longhaired. Dachshund puppies should come from litters that have only one type of coat: The different varieties are not bred to each other because they may produce puppies with shiny, mixed-up coats. There are regular-sized and miniature dogs of each coat type.

Smooth: short, sleek, and shiny two-colored—black, chocolate, wild boar, gray and fawn, with tan markings; dapple and brindle. Tail tapers to a point.

Wirehaired: short coat with soft, shorter undercoat and wiry beard and eyebrows, in any of the above colors.

Longhaired: sleek, shining, slightly wavy (not curly), in same colors as Smooth. Tail should be like a flag, with the longest hair at the base.

GERMANY

EXCERPTS FROM THE STANDARD

General Appearance:
Low to the ground, long in body and short of leg, well-balanced, bold and confident with intelligent, alert expression.

Size, Proportion, and Substance:
Miniature—11 pounds and under at 12 months of age and older.
Standard—approximately 16 to 32 pounds.

Foxhounds like children and other people and can be lovable pets, but usually they are bred for a special purpose: chasing foxes.

The first pack of foxhounds in America arrived from England on a sailing ship in 1650. George Washington had hounds from both England and France. These and other foxhounds were brought into America even before it was the United States. They are the ancestors of today's American Foxhounds.

American Foxhounds are skilled in following scents. They are generally fast, smart, strong, and friendly. Hundreds of years of pack living make them comfortable in the company of other animals. They know how to get along without being too bossy or fussy.

The Foxhound enjoys country living. He has a strong need for lots of outdoor exercise. Weekly brushing takes care of his short, thick coat, which is usually black, tan, and white, although any color is acceptable.

Fox hunting is chasing foxes with a pack of hounds while riding on horses. Today it is practiced for fun and not to control the number of foxes. Only experienced riders can "ride to hounds." The most important members of the fox hunt club wear red coats, which are called "pink." All the other riders are dressed in their finest riding clothes, usually including black coats, boots, and hats.

The hounds are guided by the huntsman into areas where foxes might live. When they pick up the scent of the fox, the hounds cry out. The leaders of the hunt shout "Tallyho!," and the chase is on. The horses gallop across the countryside after the hounds, over fields, through woods, and across streams. The fox is usually too clever to get caught, and the excitement is in the chase and a day of high-energy riding.

EXCERPTS FROM THE STANDARD

General Appearance:
Having a close, hard coat of medium length and a muscular body, there are several types within the standard.

Size, Proportion, and Substance:
Height—males, 22 to 25 inches; females, 21 to 24 inches at the withers.

USA

Foxhound, English

Most foxhounds in the United States are American Foxhounds, but there are also English Foxhounds. They are larger in bone than their American cousins, but similar in temperament. The English Foxhound is primarily a hunting hound; he may sometimes be a family pet if he has the kind of personality to fit into a life with people. Foxhounds are steady dogs, and they get along well with other animals. They have the hound's sense of smell and curiosity. Foxhounds may be in any hound color— usually they are brown, black, and white. The tail curves upward cheerfully, with slightly longer hair underneath.

ENGLAND

EXCERPTS FROM THE STANDARD

General Appearance:
Muscular but not heavy with legs as straight as posts, large bones, and a deep chest.

Size, Proportion, and Substance:
The symmetry of the Foxhound is of greatest importance.

FUN FACTS

Fox hunting has been practiced in England for hundreds of years, at least since the 1400s. Hunting larger game, such as deer, was more popular then. But starting in the late 1600s, packs of hounds were kept especially for hunting foxes. Hunting the fox grew into a national passion in Britain. It took money to raise and train the hounds and to keep hunting horses in top condition, so it was mostly a sport of the upper class. But any farmer whose land was crossed by the hunt could hop on his horse and join in the contest of man, horse, and hound in pursuit of fox.

Greyhound

Greyhounds are as fast as they are smart, as wise as they are loving. Outdoors, it is a thrill to watch this dog run at full stretch. Indoors, he becomes a quiet and dignified family member, expecting hugs and petting from his family.

Greyhounds have been speedy hunters of rabbits and other larger animals for thousands of years. They were treated to lives of luxury by the royalty of ancient Egypt; carvings of them appear in Egyptian tombs. The first written description of the breed appears in ancient Roman texts by the Roman poet Ovid. Greyhounds came to America in the early 1500s, brought by Spanish explorers.

With their tall, slim bodies, Greyhounds strike a royal figure, but they are gentle giants. The Greyhound's sleek, smooth coat feels like velvet. Any color is permitted for the breed.

EXCERPTS FROM THE STANDARD

General Appearance:
Dark, bright eyes showing intelligence and spirit; long and muscular with a deep chest and a long, fine, tapering tail that curves upward.

Size, Proportion, and Substance:
Weight—males, 65 to 70 pounds; females, 60 to 65 pounds.

AFRICA/EGYPT

FUN FACTS

The Greyhound body is designed for speed. He is the fastest dog in the world, able to reach speeds of 40 to 50 miles per hour. He is the second-fastest animal on land; only the cheetah is faster.

The sport of Greyhound racing takes place when these fleet-footed dogs follow a mechanical rabbit around a track. When the dogs retire from racing, they can be adopted by families.

Harrier

This dog looks exactly like a small English Foxhound, except that he doesn't chase foxes. He chases rabbits and hares (larger rabbits), and so is called the Harrier. He is a bit larger than his other cousin, the Beagle, but is similar to the Beagle in personality. Friendly and lovable, he's great with children.

Harriers have been in this country since colonial times, though they are rare here. They can be seen more often in Europe, where they hunt in packs. They've been doing that since at least 1260 in England.

Be prepared to give the Harrier lots of exercise. He needs action, and can go long distances. Harriers are alert and curious. They can also have minds of their own, so obedience training may require patience.

 FUN FACTS

Hare hunting is usually done by people on horseback with a pack of Harriers. But like Beagling, it can also be done following the hounds on foot. About 50 years ago in England, many less fancy packs were put together from scratch. Each person owning even one or two Harriers could bring them together to make a pack just for the hunt that day.

EXCERPTS FROM THE STANDARD

General Appearance:
Sturdily built with large bone; active, balanced, and strong. Appearing like a small English Foxhound.

Size, Proportion, and Substance:
Height—18 to 22 inches; slightly longer than high; solidly built.

ENGLAND

The Ibizan Hound is an old breed, with evidence in Egyptian tombs tracing Ibizans back to 3400 B.C. They are named after the island Ibiza, near Spain where they developed.

They were probably brought to the island by Phoenician sailors in the eighth or ninth century B.C. Here the breed survived despite hard living conditions. Ibizans were trained to become excellent rabbit hunters. This was not done for sport, but to provide food for the island people. Because food was scarce, the dogs were necessary to the survival of the people.

Ibizans are strong and healthy dogs. They are fast, and they can jump fences from a standing position. They are adaptable and affectionate family pets. Their coats are red, white, or some red-and-white combination. Ibizan hounds can have longer wiry coats and bushy moustaches.

SPAIN

EXCERPTS FROM THE STANDARD

General Appearance:
Strong and springy, with a deer-like appearance. Muscular, but not heavy.

Size, Proportion, and Substance:
Height—males, 23 1/2 to 27 1/2 inches at the whithers; females, 22 1/2 to 26 inches. Weight—males, about 50 pounds; females, about 45 pounds.

Guarding the entrance to the tomb of King Tutankhamen, wearing a heavy gold necklace, is a statue of a dog exactly like the Ibizan Hound of today. It is Anubis, Watchdog of the Dead. With his large, upright ears and long face, archaeologists used to believe the statue was a jackal. But this animal was really the gentle and friendly Ibizan Hound ancestor. The statue dates from the late 1300s B.C.

Irish Wolfhound

Years ago in the woods of Ireland lived elk so tall they measured six feet at the shoulder. There were also plenty of wolves. To hunt those animals the Irish used the gentle dog now known as the Irish Wolfhound—the largest dog alive.

Despite his size, this shaggy-coated sighthound has a peaceful and quiet personality. He is affectionate and loves to be with people. He makes a good pet because he is quiet indoors, after he has outgrown his puppy years.

Those who live with Irish Wolfhounds know that, because of their size and history as a castle breed, these dogs require a lot of food, space, and exercise. Coat color is usually gray, brindle, red, black, white, or fawn.

IRELAND

EXCERPTS FROM THE STANDARD

General Appearance:
Strong though graceful, of great size and commanding appearance.
Tail carried with an upward sweep.

Size, Proportion, and Substance:
For dogs more than 18 months:
Height—males, 32 inches or more;
females, 30 inches or more.
Weight—males, 120 pounds or more;
females, 105 pounds
or more.

FUN FACTS

The Irish Wolfhound's puppy years are something to think about. In just six months, these puppies weigh about 100 pounds. That's a lot of untrained, inexperienced dog to handle. They may be clumsy as puppies because of their size. Children can be accidentally knocked over, even though the dog really means to be playful. Future owners of Irish Wolfhounds need to be aware of these challenges.

Norwegian Elkhound

It takes a brave dog to track a moose, and that's what Norwegian Elkhounds did for thousands of years. Hunting through snowy forests with their Stone Age human companions, they would go in search of large prey—moose, elk, or bear. They worked ahead of the hunter. When they found the animal, they trapped it in a corner of underbrush, then they barked loudly to call their master.

Over the thousands of years that it has existed, the Norwegian Elkhound has looked just as it does now. Nature made him strong and clever, so he could be a good hunter. His thick, soft, gray coat can stand the cold and snow of Norway. And his noble, playful ways have made him a beloved friend. It's no wonder that the Elkhound was cherished by the Vikings. Puppies are born black and lighten as they grow.

EXCERPTS FROM THE STANDARD

General Appearance:
A hardy, medium-sized dog, square in profile with a dense gray coat, courageous and strong.

Size, Proportion, and Substance:
Height—males, 20 1/2 inches at withers females, 19 1/2 inches. Weight—males, about 55 pounds; females, about 48 pounds.

FUN FACTS

Norwegian Elkhounds have tightly curled tails and gray, silver, and black coats. Ears, muzzle, and tail tip are black. Eyes are dark brown. A stripe of black called the "harness mark" runs down his shoulders. The downy soft undercoat sheds out about twice a year. Brushing helps keep it under control, but expect lots of it. That undercoat insulates the dog against cold as well as hot weather. In winter the Norwegian Elkhound will bounce around in the snow like a kid. In summer he'll love to lie in streams and cool off.

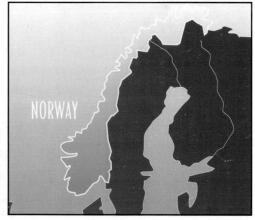

NORWAY

Otterhound

EXCERPTS FROM THE STANDARD

General Appearance:
A large, rough-coated hound showing great strength and dignity, inquisitive and persistent.

Size, Proportion, and Substance:
Height—males, 24 to 27 inches at withers; females, 23 to 26 inches. Weight—males, 75 to 115 pounds; females, 65 to 100 pounds.

ENGLAND

The Otterhound has existed since the days of knights in armor in the Middle Ages. Otters were not hunted for sport then, they were hunted because they ate the fish people wanted for themselves! Today, otter hunting is against the law, but Otterhounds are still around.

These are big dogs with big appetites. They are also strong. Because of their large size, long swishing tail, and gregarious personality, Otterhounds should live where they can get plenty of exercise. They love people.

The Otterhound has a full coat; sometimes the hair is six inches long. That means the coat needs brushing almost every day. He has long ears. He has a rough outercoat with a soft undercoat. The Otterhound is one of the rarest of the AKC breeds in America.

FUN FACTS

Like the otters they used to hunt, Otterhounds' thick, oily coats are water resistant—and Otterhounds do love water. Just getting a drink from the water bowl is swimming to some Otterhounds. They may push their whole face into the water and come up with a dripping wet beard. Their webbed feet help them swim for long distances or periods of time.

Petit Basset Griffon Vendéen

This little dog gives a whole French lesson with his big name: *Petit* means "small," *basset* means "low to the ground," *griffon* means "shaggy-faced" (about dogs, in any language), and Vendéen is the area of France that he comes from. The breed is usually nicknamed Petit or PBGV.

Petits have been known in the United States only since the 1980s. But their raggedy looks, small size, and sparky personality have won them many admirers. Though Basset is part of his name, he is not like a Basset Hound. He is more like a terrier; curious and busy, determined and smart. The Petits need plenty of exercise and attention.

The Petit carries his tail high in the air, swinging it back and forth like a sword. He has big, dark eyes and a happy, mischievous expression behind his bushy eyebrows. His coat is harsh to the touch, not soft or silky. He is mostly white with lemon, orange, black, or a mixture of colors.

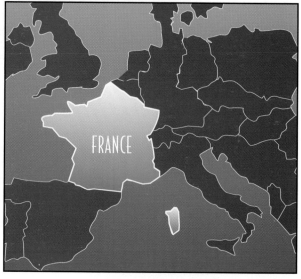

FRANCE

EXCERPTS FROM THE STANDARD

General Appearance:
A bold and lively character; compact, tough and robust. Casual in appearance, but always alert.

Size, Proportion, and Substance:
Height—males and females, 13 to 15 inches. Somewhat longer than tall.

FUN FACTS

This French hunting dog was bred to track down rabbits and other small prey. His harsh, wiry coat allows him to go into briars and brambles without getting scratched. His cousin is the Grand (large) Basset Griffon Vendéen. The Grands were used to hunt down larger prey such as deer and wolves.

Pharaoh Hound

EXCERPTS FROM THE STANDARD

General Appearance:
Medium sized, noble, graceful, and powerful; a fast runner.

Size, Proportion, and Substance:
Height—males, 23 to 25 inches; females, 21 to 24 inches.

The Pharaoh Hound's coat is a rich, warm tan color. His eyes are amber, and his nose is flesh-colored. And when the dog is really happy, his nose and eyes darken: He blushes and glows with excitement. This trait has been found in the Pharaoh dog for thousands of years. He is one of the oldest domesticated dogs in history.

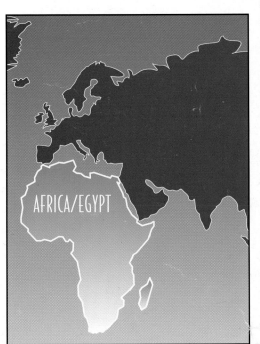

AFRICA/EGYPT

The Pharaoh Hound comes from Egypt. Pictures of him are on numerous tombs, showing that even in ancient times he was a companion and hunter. Pharaoh Hounds were buried with honor, as were their masters.

Sailing traders brought them from Egypt to the island of Malta, near Italy. There they continued to be rabbit hunters. The people loved them so much that they became the national dog of Malta, and a coin was made depicting a Pharaoh Hound.

These hounds are eager to please and can be trained easily. They get along well with other dogs. The Pharaoh Hound is a playful, active dog. He needs lots of exercise, loves attention and affection, and especially enjoys playing with children. He is an alert watchdog.

Rhodesian Ridgeback

The Rhodesian Ridgeback grew out of a combination of various breeds. Many dogs were brought to South Africa by the Europeans who moved there in the sixteenth and seventeenth centuries. These early settlers brought Danes, Mastiffs, Greyhounds, Bloodhounds, and terriers, among others.

But there were already native African dogs living in the area. One group of native people, the Hottentots, had a half-wild dog with a strange coat. A long patch of hair on his back grew in the opposite direction from the rest of his coat. It was like a long cowlick running down his back. Over the years, the Hottentot dog was bred with the European dogs to finally produce the Rhodesian Ridgeback as we know it today.

The Ridgeback was bred to hunt game—even lions—but also to guard homes and protect families. This is a strong dog, but one who wants to please. He is proud, dignified, and courageous, devoted to his family, and protective and loving of children. His short coat ranges in color from tan to chestnut.

EXCERPTS FROM THE STANDARD

General Appearance:
Strong, muscular, and active, with a ridge of hair on his back growing in the opposite direction to the rest of the coat. The ridge starts behind the shoulders and continues to a point between the hips; it should contain two identical crowns opposite each other.

Size, Proportion, and Substance:
Height—males, 25 to 27 inches; females, 24 to 26 inches. Weight—males, 75 pounds; females, 65 pounds.

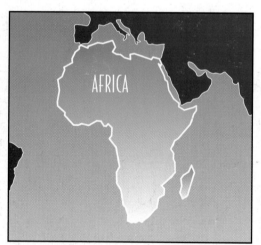

AFRICA

FUN FACTS

As a tribute to his bravery, the Rhodesian Ridgeback is also known as the African Lion Hound. The Ridgeback would find the lion and keep him in place until the hunters, following safely on horseback, arrived.

Saluki

The Saluki is related to the Afghan Hound, Borzoi, Irish Wolfhound, Scottish Deerhound, and Greyhound. All descended from the royal dog of Egypt, the beloved companion of Egyptian pharaohs and the royal family. Over the centuries these dogs developed into different breeds. Where they lived had a major effect on how they turned out. The Saluki was the dog of the Moslems, who considered him sacred. He slept in the sheik's tent. The graceful and beautiful Saluki is usually quiet indoors, but is active outdoors and needs serious exercise. This dog is fast. Because of his independent nature, training him takes patience and humor. He is devoted to his owner and does not usually warm up to strangers.

The Saluki's ears, legs, and tail have long silky hair, while the rest of the body has a short coat. His colors include white, cream, fawn, golden, red, grizzle and tan, black and tan, and tricolor (white, black, and tan).

EXCERPTS FROM THE STANDARD

General Appearance:
Graceful and speedy, strong and active, dignified, gentle, and faithful.

Size, Proportion, and Substance:
Height—males, 23 to 28 inches; females may be considerably smaller.

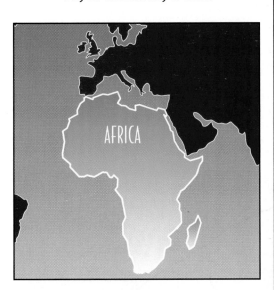

AFRICA

FUN FACTS

Because they belonged to desert tribes, Salukis developed strong resistance to the heat of the desert day and the chill of its night. Their feet are tough. They also have hair between the toes for extra protection. Because the desert tribes constantly traveled great distances, Salukis were found throughout the Middle East.

Scottish Deerhound

The Scottish Deerhound, another of the Greyhound types, became a distinct breed because of where it lived and its purpose: to hunt the large deer of the Scottish highlands. This was how the Scottish Deerhound became known as the "Royal Dog of Scotland."

The Scottish Deerhound is a quiet dog who trusts and loves people, including children. He needs human friendship and will be a devoted companion to his caring owner. He is quiet and dignified in the house. His wiry coat, with soft beard and moustache, requires a quick brushing a few times a week. He is eager to please and should be handled at all times with gentle persuasion.

He is slightly smaller and lighter in build than the Irish Wolfhound. His color is usually dark gray, but can also be light gray, yellow, red fawn or sandy red.

FUN FACTS

The Scottish Deerhound was prized during the Middle Ages for his hunting skill and courage, and for his gentle manners. During the Age of Chivalry, only nobles could own a Deerhound. If a nobleman was condemned to death, he could save himself by giving up his Deerhounds. The Deerhound was the prized companion of the Highland Chieftains, whose power ended in the 1700s when England overtook Scotland. In the following centuries the Scottish Deerhound almost became extinct, but in the twentieth century, the breed was successfully brought back.

Whippet

This graceful dog goes from sporting events to people's laps to outdoor playtime without missing a beat. Though bred to be rabbit chasers, Whippets were not the dogs of lords and ladies. Instead, coal miners in northern England developed the sport of running their dogs in a straight 200-yard race; thus, the Whippet took on the nickname of the Poor Man's Race Horse.

The Whippet is a Greyhound in miniature. The breed is only about 100 years old. Greyhounds were bred with terriers, and later Italian Greyhounds, to create this breed.

Whippets are the fastest domestic animals of their size. They can reach speeds of 35 miles per hour. But they are also quiet and well-behaved in the house. They are smart, loving, hardy little dogs who can live in the city. They can be any color. Eyes should be large and dark.

EXCERPTS FROM THE STANDARD

General Appearance:
Elegant, fit, fast, sleek, and graceful. Eyes should have a keen, alert expression.

Size, Proportion, and Substance:
Height—males, 19 to 22 inches; females, 18 to 21 inches.

So fast is the Whippet, and such a popular coursing (racing) dog, that in England he was nicknamed "the poor man's race horse." It was English mill workers who brought the dog to America and popularized Whippet racing in north central Massachusetts. From there, the sport and the breed spread. Whippet owners today enjoy participating in lure coursing events to see their quiet, dignified companions tear up the race course.

ENGLAND

WORKING DOGS

This fascinating Group has performed many jobs in history. Working dogs demonstrate how versatile and intelligent dogs can be by assisting farmers, butchers, shepherds, warriors, and nomadic tribespeople. Many have served boldly as guards.

Most of the Working dogs are large and know how to think for themselves. As an owner, it's up to you to make sure these wonderful traits are put to their most positive use. Training is essential for these dogs: They like to know what you want from them because they like to get a job done. If you don't tell them what to do, they'll be sure to come up with their own ideas.

To keep them from getting overly protective, you should socialize them early and often. Even the sweetest dogs in this group can be frightening to kids because of their large size.

The Working breeds are:

Akita	**Komondor**
Alaskan Malamute	**Kuvasz**
Bernese Mountain Dog	**Mastiff**
Boxer	**Newfoundland**
Bullmastiff	**Portuguese Water Dog**
Doberman Pinscher	**Rottweiler**
Giant Schnauzer	**Saint Bernard**
Great Dane	**Samoyed**
Great Pyrenees	**Siberian Husky**
Greater Swiss Mountain Dog	**Standard Schnauzer**

Akita

The Akita is hundreds of years old and is considered a natural treasure in his native country of Japan. The dog's image was carved on ancient Japanese tombs from the time when this majestic breed could be owned only by emperors or other nobility.

The breed was developed in the rugged, snowy mountains of northern Japan. On hunts, the Akita was trained to go after wild boars and bears, cornering them and then barking until his master arrived with a bow and arrow or spear.

Akitas arrived in America after World War II, when U.S. soldiers, who had fallen in love with the breed in Japan, brought them back to the States.

The Akita is a very strong, loyal dog who loves the company of his family and will guard them with his life. Because of his history as a guard dog, the Akita will show aggression toward other dogs, so training must begin early and must be firm, but fair.

His double coat sheds twice a year and should be brushed out twice a week.

EXCERPTS FROM THE STANDARD

General Appearance:
Large, powerful, alert, with much substance and heavy bone. Muscular, with brisk, strong movements. Dignified and courageous.

Size, Proportion, and Substance:
Height—males, 26 to 28 inches at the withers; females, 24 to 26 inches.

FUN FACTS

An example of the Akita's loyalty is the dog Hachiko. In the 1920s he lived with a Tokyo University professor. Every day he walked with his owner to the train station to see him off to work; every evening he returned to the station to greet the professor and walk him home. One day the professor didn't return on the regular train; he had died at work. But the faithful Hachiko continued to come to the station every afternoon hoping to find him. He returned, day after day, for nine years, until his own death in 1934. There is now a statue at the train station in memory of this devoted dog.

JAPAN

Alaskan Malamute

The upper western part of Alaska is the natural home of the Alaskan Malamute. It is a harsh, cold place. The tribe of native peoples there was called the Mahlemuts, which eventually became Malamute.

The Malamutes took care of their dogs because they were partners in work. The large dogs pulled heavy sleds across snow and ice. This was the only system of transportation possible for trade and the necessities of life.

The Malamute is a heavy-set dog. He is powerful and needs lots of exercise. Joining his family hiking or sledding are favorite ways for him to spend his time. The Malamute has a thick outer coat and a dense undercoat that is soft, woolly, and oily. The undercoat sheds out twice a year, and must be brushed frequently during shedding season.

EXCERPTS FROM THE STANDARD

General Appearance:
Designed to haul heavy freight, he should be heavy-boned, powerful, and tireless. Carries himself proudly with alert head and eyes. Playful and devoted.

Size, Proportion, and Substance:
Height—males, approximately 25 inches at the withers; females, approximately 23 inches. Weight—males, approximately 85 pounds; females, approximately 75 pounds.

FUN FACTS

The Alaskan Malamute is the native Alaskan sled dog. The Siberian Husky is a smaller, quicker dog that originated in northeast Asia. The Alaskan Malamute's purpose was, and still is, to haul heavy sleds. Champion Malamutes can pull over 1,000 pounds.

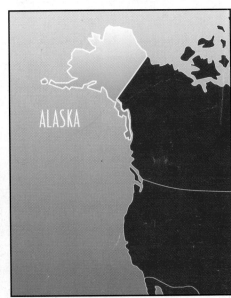

ALASKA

Bernese Mountain Dog

ernese Mountain Dogs were first brought into Switzerland over 2,000 years ago by invading Roman soldiers and established in the area of Switzerland called Berne. There, his name is Berner Sennenhund.

Just like the Swiss flag, the Bernese Mountain Dog always has a white mark in the shape of a cross on his furry chest. This big sweet dog can sometimes be shy. He forms a strong bond of love with his family, but often he attaches himself to one person.

He is eager to please and easy to train, and gets along well with other animals. He likes children, and especially enjoys pulling them in carts.

The Bernese Mountain Dog's coat is thick, long, and silky. It can be wavy or straight. He is a tricolored dog. His main color is a deep black. His markings are rich rust over his eyes, cheeks, sides of chest, on the legs, and under the tail. In summer his coat sheds, so he'll need more brushing then.

FUN FACTS

Pulling heavy loads was the original purpose of the Bernese Mountain Dog. Helping with sheep and cattle drives and guarding the barnyards were the other duties expected of this farm dog. There are three other kinds of Swiss mountain cattle dogs: Appenzeller Sennenhund, Entelbucher Sennenhund, and the Greater Swiss Mountain Dog. Only the Bernese Mountain Dog has the long silky coat.

SWITZERLAND

EXCERPTS FROM THE STANDARD

General Appearance:
Intelligent, strong, good-natured, steady, and alert. A large, sturdy, tricolored mountain dog. Full-bodied and sturdy-boned.

Size, Proportion, and Substance:
Height—males, 25 to 27 1/2 inches at the withers; females, 23 to 26 inches.

Boxer

Boxers are descended from various larger breeds, some related to Mastiffs. The breed was carefully developed in Germany using Bulldogs and some terriers. Unfortunately, Boxers were used in the cruel sports of dogfighting and bullbaiting, which are now against the law. Today, Boxers are well-mannered show dogs and loving family companions.

Boxers particularly love children. They are playful and patient, but are also strong and defensive, so early obedience training is important.

The Boxer is well known for the coat colors of fawn or brindle, both of which can be various shades. Boxers usually have some white markings and a black mask on their face. A quick weekly brushing takes care of their grooming needs.

EXCERPTS FROM THE STANDARD

General Appearance:
A squarely built, medium-sized dog with clean, hard muscles under a tight skin. Proud, agile, alert, loyal, courageous.

Size, Proportion, and Substance:
Height—males, 22 1/2 to 25 inches; females, 21 to 23 1/2 inches.

GERMANY

FUN FACTS

The Boxer is a playful and fun-loving dog, who is also capable of communicating his feelings with his face. His twinkling black eyes show his intelligence and emotions. His face wrinkles up into expressions of curiosity, excitement, happiness, surprise, or sadness. Often he copies the emotional expressions of his human companion.

Boxers were named after their habit of fighting. At the beginning of a fight with another dog, a Boxer would stand up on his hind legs and bat at his opponent, appearing to "box" with his front paws. Dogfighting is now illegal.

Bullmastiff

The Bullmastiff's name reveals his ancestry. He is part Bulldog, part Mastiff. To protect the game of large estates from poachers, English gamekeepers tried Mastiffs. They were protective, but not fast or fierce enough to catch the thieves. The Bulldog was then a ferocious dog, but not big enough to be frightening. Combining these two breeds gave them just the right dog. Dark brindle colors were considered good camouflage in the forests. Today's Bullmastiffs usually sport the soft fawn color of Mastiffs.

The Bullmastiff is a levelheaded, steady dog. He gets along well with other family pets and loves children. He is brave and protective. He saves his deep bark for really important matters.

The Bullmastiff is large and strong, so early obedience training is a must. He must learn not to pull on the leash—he easily could be stronger than the person walking him. He does well in the country or suburbs, and is polite and calm in the house.

The Bullmastiff's puppyhood can be challenging. His chewing needs are big, too. His short dense coat is suitable to any weather. Weekly brushing will keep it in order.

EXCERPTS FROM THE STANDARD

General Appearance:
Powerfully built, but active.

Size, Proportion, and Substance:
Height—males, 25 to 27 inches at the withers; females, 24 to 26 inches. Weight—males, 110 to 130 pounds; females, 100 to 120 pounds.

ENGLAND

FUN FACTS

The Bullmastiff used to be known as the Gamekeeper's Night Dog. The breed was developed in the 1800s to deal with the problem of "poaching." Poaching was when people would sneak into the forests of the rich landowners at night in search of birds and rabbits to eat.

Not wanting to get caught, poachers became extremely clever and fast. To protect their game, the landowners needed a fierce and courageous dog. They created the Bullmastiff to knock poachers to the ground and hold them in place until someone arrived. The dogs did not bite the poachers.

Doberman Pinscher

General Appearance:
Muscular and powerful, having great speed. Energetic, watchful, determined.

Size, Proportion, and Substance:
Height—males 26 to 28 inches at the withers; females, 24 to 26 inches. Height should equal length.

Dobermans have a strong protective instinct. Several Dobies have been known to go beyond their duty as family protectors. One Doberman rescued a motherless baby raccoon from the forest. He brought the raccoon, completely unharmed, to his owners, who raised it with the help of the dog.

Another family with just-hatched baby geese had a Doberman who got into the box and snuggled with the goslings to keep them warm and safe.

Doberman Pinschers combine a graceful appearance with a sharp intelligence. These are strong, quick-thinking dogs who have always served people as guardians and companions. Their ability to respond immediately to danger has made them one of the most reliable of all dogs.

The Doberman was carefully developed in Germany in the late 1800s. He gets his name from Louis Dobermann who developed the dog to accompany him on his rounds as his town's night watchman. The Doberman is a mixture of Rottweiler, German Pinscher, Black and Tan Terrier (*Pinscher* means "terrier" in German), and other local German dogs.

The Doberman has always been a working dog. During World War II he was trained to guard troops and run messages between units. Today, he is used by police as a guard dog and to sniff out criminals. In addition, he is an excellent guide dog for the blind and deaf. While Dobermans are excellent watch and guard dogs by nature, they are not solitary. They are family companions who need one-on-one attention.

The Doberman's shiny, sleek coat is usually black with rust markings on muzzle, throat, chest, legs, feet, and under tail. The ears may be cropped to stand erect or they may fall naturally.

The Schnauzer is an old breed from Germany. It can be traced back to the 1400s, and was developed by crossing the earlier Standard Schnauzer with a variety of other dogs. The Germans admired the Standard Schnauzer, but needed a larger dog to help them drive cattle and sheep to the markets. So they bred bigger dogs to the Standard—including the black Great Dane and some local cattle and sheep dogs.

The Giant Schnauzer's main occupation today is as a police dog. He is a bold, strong, smart dog who does best with a serious, experienced, and confident owner. With solid obedience training, he will reward you with loyalty and obedience.

The Giant Schnauzer has a dense, wiry coat, either black or salt and pepper. It requires professional grooming twice a year, and twice-weekly combing and brushing. Ears may be cropped or natural. The tail is docked.

EXCERPTS FROM THE STANDARD

General Appearance:
A larger and more powerful version of the Standard Schnauzer. Bold, composed, easily trained, playful, with a rugged and weather-resistant coat.

Size, Proportion, and Substance:
Height—males, 25 1/2 to 27 1/2 inches at the withers; females, 23 1/2 to 25 1/2 inches.

FUN FACTS

Schnauzers today are divided into three separate breeds: the Miniature, the Standard, and the Giant. The Miniature is the newest and the Standard is the oldest. They were all developed in the region of Bavaria, Germany, for different purposes.

GERMANY

The Great Dane is often referred to as the king of dogs. By looking at him, it's easy to see why.

A giant, dignified dog of sweet and gentle nature but also of mighty power, the Great Dane is an old breed. And even though Dane means Danish, the dog was developed in Germany at least 400 years ago, where his purpose was to hunt down the wild boar, a ferocious and tough beast. Now the Great Dane's job is to be a devoted and wonderful friend.

Because he is large, he needs a lot of space and exercise. In the house, he's calm and well behaved. Another important fact is that this big fellow eats plenty of food.

The Great Dane is a quick learner in obedience school, and needs the training because he's strong enough to pull his owner behind him. He won't do that if he's trained to walk properly. He wants to please.

FUN FACTS

Great Danes come in five colors: brindle (gold with black stripes); fawn (gold with black on the face); blue (a blue-gray steel color); black; or harlequin. A harlequin is a clown whose costume is all black-and-white diamond shapes. A harlequin Great Dane is mostly white, with black patches over most of his body. The neck should be white. Great Danes' ears may be cropped or left to fall naturally.

EXCERPTS FROM THE STANDARD

General Appearance:
A majestic, dignified, elegant dog. Powerful, smooth, and strong.

Size, Proportion, and Substance:
Height—male, 30 to 32 or more inches at the withers; females, 28 to 30 or more inches.

GERMANY

Great Pyrenees

A range of rugged mountains lies along the border between France and Spain. It was here, in the Pyrenees Mountains, that the Great Pyrenees dog was developed to protect sheep.

Wild wolves and bears roamed the mountainsides in search of food, but they couldn't get past the Great Pyrenees dog. This big, brave dog was devoted to his flock and courageous against attackers. He was protected by his thick coat and usually wore a collar with sharp metal spikes.

Because of his size, the Great Pyrenees is a lot of dog to handle, and needs plenty of space at home. Usually he is calm and serious. He forms deep, loving attachments to his family that last a lifetime. Sometimes he chooses one person as his special friend. To strangers, he can seem independent.

Something to think about is the beautiful white coat of the Great Pyrenees. As big as a snow drift, it requires brushing only once or twice a week, but each time it takes one to two hours to comb it out correctly. In spring, when the winter coat sheds out, plan on even more brushing.

FRANCE

FUN FACTS

Since wolves and bears are not so numerous now in France and Spain, the Great Pyrenees has taken on additional duties. He is eager to pull carts and sleds. He guides passengers along snowy trails: He can find the dangerous spots and lead people away from them. He carried equipment in sacks across his back in World War I, and he was used by smugglers to take illegal goods between France and Spain.

EXCERPTS FROM THE STANDARD

General Appearance:
Possessing a kindly, regal expression, great strength, and elegance.

Size, Proportion, and Substance:
Height—males, 27 to 32 inches at the withers; females, 25 to 29 inches. Weight—for a 27-inch male, about 100 pounds; for a 25-inch female, about 85 pounds.

Descended from the Mastiffs of ancient Rome, the Greater Swiss Mountain Dog is a dog of majesty and dignity. His history, however, is not a royal one. He has quietly made his reputation by centuries of hard work for the farmers and villagers of the Swiss Alps.

The "Swissie" was used mainly as a cattle-driving dog, and was the most common dog in the Alps until the late 1800s. Swissie owners allowed their dogs to interbreed with dogs belonging to friends and neighbors. The working ability of the dogs, and not their appearance, was the only breeding consideration. Rottweilers and Saint Bernards were likely part of some of these interbreedings.

The Swissie has a thick neck, broad chest, and muscular thighs. It is a sturdy, full-bodied and alert dog, never clumsy. As a member of a family, he is gentle and calm, loving and obedient.

The Swissie's coat is always short, but his markings are like the Bernese Mountain Dog's—mostly black, with white on the chest, face, tail, and feet. His thick, double coat requires once- or twice-weekly brushing. Nose is always black; eyes are never blue.

EXCERPTS FROM THE STANDARD

General Appearance:
A striking, tricolored, large, powerful dog; sturdy enough to pull loads.

Size, Proportion, and Substance:
Height—males, 25 1/2 to 28 1/2 inches at the withers; females, 23 1/2 to 27 inches.

SWITZERLAND

FUN FACTS

The Greater Swiss Mountain Dog was not considered a specific breed until the early 1900s. In 1908, two Swissies were entered in a dog show as "short-haired Bernese Mountain Dogs." The judge declared that the dogs should be a separate and distinct breed, which he named the Grosser Schweizer Sennenhund, or Greater Swiss Mountain Dog. The first Swissies came into the United States in 1968. But the breed is still small in numbers, even in Switzerland. The Greater Swiss Mountain Dog is the largest and probably oldest of the Swiss mountain cattle-driving dogs.

Komondor

EXCERPTS FROM THE STANDARD

General Appearance:
A big, muscular dog with plenty of bone and substance, covered with an unusual, heavy white coat.

Size, Proportion, and Substance:
Height—males, 25 1/2 or more at withers; females, 23 1/2 inches or more.

FUN FACTS

The Komondor's most unique feature is his coat. Some say he looks like a mop. When he's a puppy, his coat is soft and woolly. Then, when he reaches about two years old, it grows naturally into "cords." As the stronger hair of his outer coat grows in, it becomes wrapped in the softer undercoat to form the cords. To keep the dog looking top-notch, the cords need to be separated by hand. Washing the coat is a major event. After washing, the cords must be carefully rinsed, and the coat should be blown dry. Washing can take an hour; drying can take four to eight hours. The plural of Komondor is Komondorok.

The Komondor is a serious dog who loves the outdoors. Although he is mostly a family pet in this country, he was a guardian of sheep and cattle in his native Hungary. He is descended from herding dogs found on the rugged plains of Russia and brought to Hungary in the fifth century.

The Komondor was not required to herd the sheep or to do any work except stand guard over the flock or herd. The busy work was left to other dogs. The Komondor's stern and watchful eye kept most predators away. But when challenged by an attacker, the Komondor has always been a fearless fighter. His three best weapons are his massive strength, his thick, corded coat, and his sharp thinking.

Knowing the Komondor's background helps explain his personality today. He can think for himself, since his ancestors usually protected the sheep with no people nearby. These qualities mean he does best in a family that knows how to handle a bold dog who needs plenty of room to run.

HUNGARY

Kuvasz

The Kuvasz is similar in appearance to the Great Pyrenees. They are both probably descended from dogs of Tibet, but the Kuvasz developed in Hungary instead of France.

The Kuvasz was originally the dog of kings, especially King Mattias I, ruler of Hungary from 1458 to 1490, but eventually Kuvaszok (plural for Kuvasz) were owned by regular citizens, too. They were developed into skillful guardians of sheep and cattle. This is the work they do today.

The Kuvasz is a protective dog. He is brave, strong, and suspicious of strangers. But when he makes a friend, it's for life. He is extra protective of children. Obedience training is important. The Kuvasz needs space and exercise in large amounts. But he also needs loving attention from his family, to whom he is devoted. He may not always show it on the outside, but he longs for his family's affection.

The Kuvasz's coat is thick, long, and white. It sheds year round, even with twice-weekly brushing.

FUN FACTS

To ensure a close connection with the flocks they protect, working Kuvasz puppies are raised with the baby lambs. The soft, woolly white bundles grow up together, devoted friends. They form a deep attachment to each other. The lambs trust the dogs completely. And the dogs feel completely responsible for the sheep.

EXCERPTS FROM THE STANDARD

General Appearance:
A large working dog, sturdily built; white with no markings; well muscled without bulkiness. Moves freely, showing strength and activity.

Size, Proportion, and Substance:
Height—males, 28 to 30 inches at the withers; females, 26 to 28 inches. Weight—males, approximately 100 to 115 pounds; females, 70 to 90 pounds.

HUNGARY

Mastiff

When the Romans invaded Britain in 55 B.C., Caesar noticed a powerful, fearless breed of dog that fought beside the British soldiers. He was so impressed by the strength and courage of these dogs that he brought some back to Rome with him, where they were forced to take part in sports such as bull and bearbaiting, even fighting against lions.

This dog was the Mastiff and has been raised in Britain for more than 2,000 years. The Mastiff is one of the biggest, bulkiest dogs of all—some can top 200 pounds. But the Mastiff is a gentle friend to man by nature, always serving as man's watchdog and loyal companion. This is a dog who likes being around people. He needs their company and bonds closely with his family. He takes his time, doing things with a great majesty and steady character.

Because of his large size, he needs room to move. He is best suited to life in the country or suburbs. Mastiffs have a massive head set in a large body. The coat is short and thick fawn or brindle.

EXCERPTS FROM THE STANDARD

General Appearance:
A large, massive dog, showing grandeur and dignity. Heavy boned.

Size, Proportion, and Substance:
Height—males, 30 inches or more at the withers; females, 27 1/2 inches or more.

FUN FACTS

Mastiffs are renowned for their loyalty. In 1415, Sir Peers Legh, an English knight, traveled to France for the Battle of Agincourt. He was wounded and fell to the ground. His faithful Mastiff stood guard over him for hours, defending him against attackers. Finally English soldiers were able to rescue the fallen knight and take him to Paris. Sir Peers did not survive his wounds, but his Mastiff was taken back to her master's castle in England to live out her days. There is still a stained glass window in the castle showing Sir Peers with his devoted Mastiff.

ENGLAND

Newfoundland

Fishermen from France, Spain, and Portugal first brought the white Great Pyrenees to the Canadian island of Newfoundland during their travels. Over the generations, the dog was bred with other local dogs to create a fisherman's true friend: the Newfoundland. These dogs were kept busy hauling in the heavy fishing nets, pulling carts, and carrying loads in big bags. But they also became renowned for their steadfast bravery in rescue work. They have carried life lines to sinking ships in seas no boat or man could cross. And they have saved countless children and adults from drowning by swimming with them safely to shore.

Most important in Newfoundlands is their temperament. Their kindly expression is calm, patient and dignified. They need human companionship to be happy. They love children.

Because of their size, "Newfs" need room to move, and love a place to swim. His coat should be brushed everyday, especially during shedding season. Shade and extra water are essential in the summer. Black is the usual color, though some Newfoundlands are brown, gray, or black-and-white (called "Landseer").

EXCERPTS FROM THE STANDARD

General Appearance:
A sweet-dispositioned dog, at home on land and in water; large, heavily coated, deep-bodied, heavily boned, muscular and strong, with dignity and pride.

Size, Proportion, and Substance:
Height—males, approximately 28 inches at the withers; females, approximately 26 inches. Weight—males, 130 to 150 pounds; females, 100 to 120 pounds.

FUN FACTS

The English poet Lord Byron was so fond of his Newfoundland, Boatswain, that he built a monument to him when he died, with this poem on it:

Near this spot
are deposited the Remains of one
who possessed Beauty without Vanity,
Strength without Insolence,
Courage without Ferocity,
and all the Virtues of Man without his Vices.
This Praise, which would be unmeaning Flattery
if inscribed over human Ashes,
is but a just tribute to the Memory of
BOATSWAIN, a DOG,
who was born in Newfoundland May 1803
and died at Newstead Nov. 18th, 1808.

NEWFOUNDLAND

Portuguese Water Dog

The Portuguese Water Dog is a lively, fun-loving dog who is gaining popularity because of his nonshedding coat. At one time the Portuguese Water Dog was critically important to the fishermen of Portugal, but he almost became extinct when modern commercial fishing methods made this intelligent dog's job obsolete.

Originating in Asia, when the Portugese Water Dog's ancestors were brought into Europe it was believed they developed into various dogs: In Germany, they became the Poodle; in Ireland, they became the Irish Water Spaniel. In Portugal, they were put to work in the water to herd fish into nets, and became the Portuguese Water Dog.

The hardworking, seaworthy history of Portuguese Water Dogs shows up in the breed of today. The dog is adaptable to any living situation—city or country—as long as he gets enough exercise. He is loaded with energy and doesn't tire easily. He is highly trainable, and water, of course, is his favorite place to play.

FUN FACTS

The Portuguese Water Dog has a thick, even coat, with no undercoat. It can be either curly or wavy. It does not shed, but it does require care. Two clips are standard. The Retriever Clip gives a natural appearance. The coat is clipped overall to a length of one inch. A plume of long hair is left at the end of the tail. In the Lion Clip, the middle and hindquarters of the dog, as well as his muzzle, are clipped short while his front half (except the face) and tail tip are left a full, shaggy length. Either clip is acceptable in the show ring. The coat comes in black, white, brown, or white with black nose, mouth, and eyelids.

PORTUGAL

Rottweiler

The Rottweiler is originally descended from the Mastiff-type dogs of Asia, and is thought to have originated with the Romans, who brought the dog with them as a guard dog and drover, or cattle driver, on their expeditions across Europe.

The Rottweiler is both a bold guardian and an intelligent, steady friend. But he is rather aloof, owing to his history as a hardworking drover and guardian. With his owner, though, he aims to accompany and guard with all his heart. His great strength should be channeled into positive activities. He loves exercise and will thrill to the challenges of any outdoor sports that include dog and owner.

The Rottweiler's coat, which needs brushing once a week, is always black with rust markings.

EXCERPTS FROM THE STANDARD

General Appearance:
A robust and powerful dog, showing great strength, agility, confidence, and endurance.

Size, Proportion, and Substance:
Height—males, 24 to 27 inches at the withers; females, 22 to 25 inches.

FUN FACTS

The name of this breed comes from the town of Rottweil, Germany, where the dog was developed. Its meaning in German is "red tile," because the town originally had a Roman settlement of red-tiled houses.

GERMANY

Saint Bernard

For hundreds of years, Saint Bernards have been renowned for their bravery in rescue work, saving thousands of lives in the treacherous mountains of the Alps between Switzerland and Italy. At the same time, Saint Bernards have been just as well known for their big, loving personalities.

The breed was traditionally the companion of monks who lived in hospices high in the Swiss Alps. When a person was lost in the snowy mountain passes, the Saint Bernards were used to find the unlucky traveler. Their keen sense of smell and pathfinding skills, combined with their durability in the cold, made them life-saving naturals.

These early rescuers were short-haired Saint Bernards; the longhaired variety appeared in the 1830s when the breed was crossed with the Newfoundland to create a variety used mostly as a farm dog.

Both kinds of coats need brushing weekly, daily during shedding. Colors are white with red, brown-yellow, or brindle.

FUN FACTS

To train for rescue work, young Saint Bernards would go out on mountain searches with monks and older dogs. When the missing person was located, the young dog lay down beside the person to warm him and lick his face so the person wouldn't fall asleep and freeze to death. The older dogs went back to the hospice, alerted a search party, and guided searches back to the lost person.

EXCERPTS FROM THE STANDARD

General Appearance:
Powerful, strong, and tall, intelligent expression.

Size, Proportion, and Substance:
Height—males, 27 1/2 inches or taller at the withers; females, 25 inches or taller.

SWITZERLAND

Samoyed

FUN FACTS

In 1911, Roald Amundsen of Norway was the first man to reach the South Pole. He got there by dog sled, pulled by a team of Samoyeds. Only one other dog sled team has been to Antarctica. That was in 1990. Now dogs are banned from the South Pole because scientists decided that the area was endangered and dogs could bring diseases such as distemper to seals and other wildlife historically unexposed to dogs.

FINLAND   MONGOLIA

Samoyeds are perky, dependable playmates, often wearing "smiles" on their faces. They are full of fun, and love nothing more than an afternoon of frisky activity in the snow. They are active and alert, indoors and out.

The Samoyed was beloved by the Samoyed people, a tribe that roamed the icy tundra near the Arctic Ocean. He is considered the oldest of the Arctic breeds, and has a tough make-up as a result. He was a necessary part of the Samoyed life: guarding the tribe's reindeer, pulling heavy sleds, and accompanying his people everywhere. Being so close to people for thousands of years, Samoyeds are loving companions.

The Samoyed has a strikingly beautiful coat, shiny and white as the Arctic plains. It can also be white and biscuit, cream, or all biscuit. It is a double coat, a harsh outer coat with a soft woolly undercoat. The undercoat keeps the dog warm in winter and protects him from too much heat in summer. The coat sheds twice a year.

Siberian Husky

The Siberian Husky is an outgoing, fun-loving dog. He is lighter in build than the Alaskan Malamute, and also less bold. But he still requires an alert owner who stays in control, as the Siberian's nature is to roam and explore, as his Arctic ancestors did.

The breed was developed by the Chukchi tribe of northeastern Asia as a sled dog, and had to pull sleds for the tribe over the vast, frozen countryside in search of food.

Siberian Huskies appeared in Alaska early in the 1900s, and were used for Arctic expeditions. They were also part of the Army's Arctic Search and Rescue Unit during World War II.

The Husky has a double coat, and when the soft undercoat sheds, it "blows." That is, it comes out in fuzzy clumps all over. Brushing every day during these times is a must. The coat is medium length and soft. All colors are permitted. Siberians have brown or blue eyes, and sometimes one of each.

EXCERPTS FROM THE STANDARD

General Appearance:
Friendly, interested, mischievous; a medium-sized working dog, quick and light on his feet, graceful.

Size, Proportion, and Substance:
Height—males, 21 to 23 1/2 inches at the withers; females, 20 to 22 inches. Weight—males, 45 to 60 pounds; females, 35 to 50 pounds.

FUN FACTS

Of all the races Siberian Huskies have run, none was more important than the Nome Serum Run of 1925. This was a race for life. There was an outbreak of the fatal disease diphtheria in Nome, Alaska and doctors quickly ran out of the serum that could save lives and stop the spread of the disease. No planes were available to take the supply of fresh serum from Nenana to Nome—a distance of 658 miles. The trip normally took 25 days by sled. Dogs and men worked together night and day in relay teams. Miraculously, they managed the trip in just five and a half days

Standard Schnauzer

The Standard Schnauzer originated in Germany. The first of the three Schnauzer breeds—Standard, Giant, and Miniature—he has existed for hundreds of years. He is probably descended from a combination of German Poodle, gray wolf spitz, and Pinscher.

EXCERPTS FROM THE STANDARD

General Appearance:
A robust, heavyset dog; sturdy with good muscle and plenty of bone; square-built, rugged, with a dense, harsh coat, arched eyebrows, and a bristly moustache and whiskers.

Size, Proportion, and Substance:
Ideal height—males, 18 1/2 to 19 1/2 inches at the withers; females, 17 1/2 to 18 1/2 inches.

GERMANY

FUN FACTS

The Standard Schnauzer used to be classified as a terrier. But because he was so frequently a working dog in Germany, he was put into that category. This versatile dog has been used to catch rats, guard farm carts, carry messages during wars, assist the Red Cross, and serve with the police. He also can retrieve, as well as guard sheep and cattle.

The Standard Schnauzer is a mid-sized dog who is devoted to his family and has a mischievous sense of humor. He is adaptable to various living situations and can do well in the city if given enough exercise. Such a vigorous dog needs to be kept busy with positive activity. Obedience training and other dog-people games suit this dog well. It's especially important for children to participate in the obedience training of the Schnauzer to set the relationship on the right footing.

A properly groomed Standard Schnauzer will not shed much. His bristly beard and moustache need brushing or combing twice a week. His coat must be professionally groomed every few months. Colors are black or pepper-and-salt (black and white). Ears may be cropped or left natural. The tail is docked.

TERRIERS

Some terriers are small, but that doesn't stop them from being brave. They are scrappy little hunters who seek out vermin such as rats. *Terra* means "earth" in Latin; terriers are, literally, "earthdogs." They'll dig anywhere if it means catching their prey. This hunting instinct, however, can lead to digging in the yard. You can train your terrier to dig in his own special sandbox—he'll love it.

Terriers are able to live quite happily in the city or the country. Their strong sense of determination requires some determination from you when it comes to training, but your efforts will be rewarded with these clever, hardy dogs.

Many of the terriers have unique coats that don't shed. Their coats do, however, need grooming—often special trimming or clipping—to keep them looking their best.

The Terriers are:

Airedale Terrier	**Manchester Terrier**
American Staffordshire Terrier	**Miniature Bull Terrier**
Australian Terrier	**Miniature Schnauzer**
Bedlington Terrier	**Norfolk Terrier**
Border Terrier	**Norwich Terrier**
Bull Terrier	**Scottish Terrier**
Cairn Terrier	**Sealyham Terrier**
Dandie Dinmont Terrier	**Skye Terrier**
Fox Terrier (Smooth and Wire)	**Soft Coated Wheaten Terrier**
Irish Terrier	**Staffordshire Bull Terrier**
Kerry Blue Terrier	**Welsh Terrier**
Lakeland Terrier	**West Highland White Terrier**

The handsome and dignified Airedale, the largest terrier breed, has a hardworking history. Developed in Yorkshire, England, near the Aire River, he is the result of a cross between the early Black-and-Tan Terrier mixed with the larger Otterhound. He was expected to hunt down foxes, badgers, weasels, otters, and water rats.

Noble and bold, but also kindhearted, the Airedale likes to make friends with people; playing with children gives him great joy. Airedales are high-energy dogs, but they can be perfectly happy in the city if given lots of exercise. That means more than just being in the backyard with a ball and a bone: They love human company. They are also protective and like to be "top dog" in the family. For that reason, they make great watchdogs.

The Airedale has a wiry coat that needs clipping every few months; or it can be allowed to grow out into its woolly, natural shape. He is a tan dog with a dark midsection, sometimes with white on his chest.

ENGLAND

EXCERPTS FROM THE STANDARD

General Appearance:
Sturdy, well muscled.

Size, Proportion, and Substance:
Height—males, 23 inches at the withers; females, slightly less.

FUN FACTS

Airedales have great courage and have been used to hunt big game in Africa and India. They were among the first breeds used as police dogs in Germany and Great Britain. And they have been dependable message carriers in several wars, able to get information delivered fearlessly, even when injured.

American Staffordshire Terrier

The American Staffordshire Terrier is a medium-size dog, yet he is believed to be one of the strongest of all dogs. A cross between a terrier and the Bulldog, he combines the best qualities of each: the gameness and spirit of the terrier and the courage and boldness of a Bulldog.

The AmStaf was bred to be a fighting dog in the nineteenth century, but the only qualities his breeders were taking advantage of were his courage and strength. The breed is by nature a calm and quiet dog, who loves his family with all his heart and guards them just as dearly. He is famous for being able to sense the difference between friendly strangers and unwanted intruders.

He loves to play fetch and other energetic games, but looks forward to a daily walk. Families will find him an affectionate, intelligent, and protective companion.

The American Staffordshire Terrier was once considered an "all-American" dog. In fact, in World War I an AmStaf named Stubby earned the rank of sergeant and was the most decorated dog of the war. In the early 1900s, *Life* magazine frequently featured this breed.

EXCERPTS FROM THE STANDARD

General Appearance:
Great strength for his size, muscular, but agile and graceful; alert and aware of his surroundings; stocky and courageous.

Size, Proportion, and Substance:
Height—males, about 18 to 19 inches at the withers; females, about 17 to 18 inches.

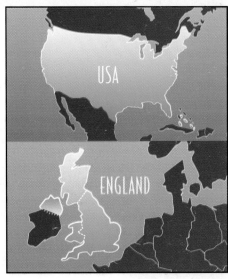

Australian Terrier

Though one of the smallest terriers, the rugged Australian Terrier was developed in the harsh conditions of the Australian Outback, where he worked side by side with the pioneers—controlling rats and snakes, alerting humans to intruders, even tending sheep. He's ready for any situation. With that easy self-confidence comes his readiness to enjoy a good friendship.

The Australian Terrier repays your attentions with a steady devotion. Since he considers himself part of the family, the Aussie gets along well with other animals and with children.

He has a double coat: a harsh outer coat and a softer undercoat. The colors are blue and tan, solid sandy, and solid red. The lighter hair on the top of his head stands up in a natural silky brush. He has naturally upstanding ears and a docked tail.

In 1868, the Australian Terrier was the first Australian breed of dog to be officially recognized by that country.

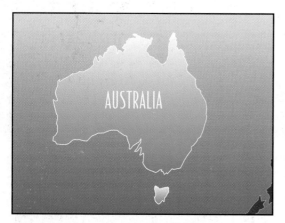

AUSTRALIA

FUN FACTS

So important is this dog's temperament (disposition) to breeders of the Australian Terrier, that they consider shyness or aggression toward people a fault of the breed. These dogs are keen, intelligent, spirited, and self-assured, but never spooky or mean.

EXCERPTS FROM THE STANDARD

General Appearance:
A small, sturdy working terrier, possessing a harsh, straight coat with a silky topknot. Expression is keen and intelligent; manner is spirited and self-assured.

Size, Proportion, and Substance:
Height—10 to 11 inches at withers.

Bedlington Terrier

The most distinctive feature of this gutsy terrier is his curly, woolly coat. He is sometimes described as having the head of a lamb and the heart of a lion. This is a dog that was bred to quickly kill not only rats, but also badgers, otters, and foxes.

The Bedlington Terrier appears outwardly to be calmer or milder than some other terriers. He isn't fussy or mischievous, and is independent in his ways. But once excited for play, he makes a quick and speedy playmate for children. He is also loving and has a big heart.

His soft coat is dark in puppyhood, but within a few months lightens dramatically to a pale bluish gray, sandy, or liver. It stands out crisply from his body in a combination of hard and soft hairs, and needs regular, professional grooming to get his clip just right, especially around his head.

ENGLAND

EXCERPTS FROM THE STANDARD

General Appearance:
The expression is mild and gentle; the action is springy and full of energy and courage; he is able to gallop at great speeds.

Size, Proportion, and Substance:
Height—males, 16½ at the withers; females, 15½. Weight—between 17 to 23 pounds.

FUN FACTS

The Bedlington Terrier was the coal miners' dog. When these men were not working down in the mines, they loved to race their Bedlingtons. Racing Whippets was also popular. The two breeds are fast runners and have similar, gracefully shaped bodies. Some believe the Bedlington looks like a Whippet in sheep's clothing.

Border Terrier

The Border Terrier gets his name because he comes from the border area between England and Scotland. There this alert and plucky dog was developed especially to catch the foxes that caused so much damage to farmers' chickens and other livestock.

The Border Terrier's soft, warm undercoat is protected from briars and brambles by a harsh and wiry outer coat. He was bred to have longer legs than most terriers. That's because he often needed to be able to keep up with horses in pursuit of the fox.

But this dog is also adaptable to city life, provided he gets plenty of exercise. He's most interested in being with his owner, and is a good-natured and loving companion who will be eager for your praise in obedience class.

The Border Terrier's coat should be brushed twice a week. His colors are red, grizzle and tan, blue and tan, or wheaten.

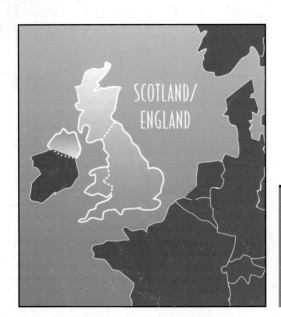

SCOTLAND/
ENGLAND

EXCERPTS FROM THE STANDARD

General Appearance:
His body is always alert, showing a fearless determination; he is active and agile, affectionate and obedient.

Size, Proportion, and Substance:
Weight—males, 13 to 15 1/2 pounds; females, 11 1/2 to 14 pounds.

FUN FACTS

The Border Terrier has a head shape that is unique among terriers. It is called an "otter" head because its shape is like that of the otter's—boxier than most terriers, with a shorter, sloping forehead, flatter face, and shorter muzzle.

Bull Terrier

Like the American Staffordshire Terrier and the Staffordshire Bull Terrier, the Bull Terrier was originally created to be a fighting dog by breeding the white English Terrier (now extinct) to the Bulldog. This produced the Bull-and-Terrier dog. Some Spanish Pointer was added to make the dog larger, and the result was the Bull Terrier.

Fortunately, dogfighting is illegal in our time, but the Bull Terrier is still valued—as a loyal and loving friend. Because they are so muscular, Bull Terriers need plenty of exercise to stay fit, and love nothing more than playing catch with a bouncy rubber ball. They make the most delightful of companions—in the city or country.

The Bullie has a distinctive face. From the side it looks like an egg. It is long, strong, and deep, curving downward from the top of the skull to the top of the nose. His forehead is flat between the ears. He has little black eyes and a black nose. In the white Bullie, there can be another color on the head.

EXCERPTS FROM THE STANDARD

General Appearance:
Strongly built, muscular, and active; full of fire, but with a sweet disposition and responsive to commands. (There is no size requirement for this breed, but males usually weigh 55-70 pounds; females 45-60 pounds.)

FUN FACTS

Among Bull Terriers, white became the favorite color in the 1860s. Now the white Bull Terrier and the "colored" Bull Terrier (any color other than white) are two varieties within the breed.

ENGLAND

Cairn Terrier

This peppy dog with the bottle-brush face was originally a friend to farmers. Even though he's small, he eagerly kept the farms of Scotland free from the predators of the farmers' livestock: otters, foxes, and rats.

The Cairn is closely related to the Scottish and West Highland White Terriers. All come from Scotland, and they often came from the same litters. Earlier in their histories, the types were defined as different from each other by color only.

Though the Cairn is small, he's not much for the pampered life. He is likely to wriggle out of laps or long hugs. He prefers to explore and play lively games, and can be equally happy in the city or on the farm. Ultimately, the Cairn deeply desires to be a part of his beloved family, even if he does seem independent at times.

The Cairn Terrier's wiry coat could blend with the Scottish landscape of rocks, heathers, and brush. Its colors include tans, browns, and grays, often with black sprinkled in.

FUN FACTS

A *cairn* is a small monument made of stones piled into a mound. In Scotland, these were traditionally created as memorials to family members. They were also landmarks to guide travelers. Cairns provided handy places for small mammals to hide after robbing henhouses or granaries. Farmers trained their terriers to invade the cairns to get at their "enemies." The dog Toto in the movie *The Wizard of Oz* was a Cairn.

EXCERPTS FROM THE STANDARD

General Appearance:
An active, fearless, sturdy, but small terrier; strong but not heavy.

Size, Proportion, and Substance:
Height—males, 10 inches at the withers; females, 9 1/2 inches. Weight—males, 14 pounds; females, 13 pounds. Length from chest to tail—14 1/2 to 15 inches. These are the ideal sizes at two years of age.

SCOTLAND

Dandie Dinmont Terrier

Don't let his big dark eyes and fluffy head of curls fool you. The Dandie Dinmont Terrier is a confident and intelligent little terrier, brave and independent. He'd rather be sergeant of the house than be babied.

This terrier comes from the same area as the Border Terrier, the hilly border between Scotland and England. He is a tough little dog first written of as a breed around 1700. He was known for his skill in getting otters and badgers.

This delightful and entertaining dog is a clown as a companion. But as a terrier, he has his pride, and can sometimes seem shy or uninterested in strangers.

Dandie Dinmonts come in two colors, pepper and mustard. Pepper is various grays; mustard ranges from reddish brown to pale fawn. Both coats are lightest on the topknot and ears.

SCOTLAND/ ENGLAND

FUN FACTS

In 1814 Sir Walter Scott wrote an adventure novel called *Guy Mannering*, which became a popular sensation. The farmer, a unique and funny character in the story, was named Dandie Dinmont. His six dogs were Auld ("old") Pepper, Auld Mustard, Young Pepper, Young Mustard, Little Pepper, and Little Mustard. Since that time, the breed of dog has always been called Dandie Dinmont.

EXCERPTS FROM THE STANDARD

General Appearance:
A long, low terrier with a curved outline having a distinctive head with a large silky topknot.

Size, Proportion, and Substance:
Height—8 to 10 inches at the withers. Weight—18 to 24 pounds.

Fox Terriers (Smooth and Wire)

Fox Terriers are lively little dogs—busy, bouncy, alert, and always ready for action. The Fox Terrier is loads of fun for older children who can give him daily play and exercise. He has a saucy manner and a happy sense of humor.

Smooth and Wire Fox Terriers are considered two separate breeds now, but used to be considered varieties within the same breed. The Smooth was the first to come along, perhaps as early as 1790. His ancestors were the smooth-coated Black-and-Tan Terrier, the Bull Terrier, the Greyhound, and the Beagle. The Wire's major ancestor was the rough-coated Black-and-Tan Terrier. Both share origins with the Airedale, Irish, and Welsh Terriers. Both are adaptable to city or country living.

Their most obvious difference, of course, is the coat. Both are predominantly white with black and tan areas. But the Smooth has a short, thick coat that needs only a quick brushing once a week. The Wire's coat is crinkled and wiry with a soft undercoat. He needs brushing twice weekly and clipping every few months.

FUN FACTS

Fox Terriers began their careers in a tough job. They were participants in the sport of fox hunting. British men and women, mounted on horseback, would chase foxes across the countryside. Fox Terriers were carried along in cloth bags or baskets by some of the riders. If the fox went down a hole or into brush where the hounds couldn't get it, the Fox Terriers were released and sent underground to scare out the fox. The dogs needed to be quick, strong, and brave in their encounters with these foxes.

Smooth

Wire

Both dogs have black noses and small, round, wide-awake black eyes. Their legs are longer than those of most other terriers their size.

SCOTLAND/ENGLAND

EXCERPTS FROM THE STANDARDS

General Appearance:
Smooth Fox Terrier—lively and active as well as powerful. Wire Fox Terrier—alert, quick, on the tip-toe of expectation.

Size, Proportion, and Substance:
Height—not to exceed 15 1/2 inches at the withers; females slightly smaller than males. Weight—about 18 pounds; females slightly less.

Irish Terrier

The Irish Terrier is a loyal and friendly dog. He has cheerfully fulfilled many jobs in his history: keeping farms free of rats, woodchucks, and rabbits; retrieving game from land and water with hunters, and hunting big game throughout the world. During World War I he even saved lives by guarding campsites and carrying messages through enemy lines. His nickname is the Daredevil.

The Irish Terrier is one of the oldest of the terrier breeds. He bears many similarities to the Airedale, Welsh, and Wire Fox Terriers and is every bit as smart and quick.

This dog can't be beat as an overall pal. He'll hardily adapt to any situation, which proves his deep loyalty to his owner. Not only will he be an enthusiastic playmate for children, he'll guard them and the home with fierce determination and pluck.

The Irish Terrier's coat is short overall and grows together tightly. He should be all of one color—bright red, golden red, red wheaten, or wheaten. Irish Terriers' tails are docked by about one quarter, and their ears are left natural.

IRELAND

EXCERPTS FROM THE STANDARD

General Appearance:
Active, graceful, sturdy, and strong.

Size, Proportion, and Substance:
Height—approximately 18 inches at the withers. Weight—males, 27 pounds; females, 25 pounds.

FUN FACTS

Most breeds' origins are shrouded in mystery, but it is the Irish Terrier's that is perhaps the most colorful. Legend has it that his first playmates were the "Little People who dance in magic rings on moonlit nights" (Irish faeries). The story goes that the Irish's curiosity led him astray. Lost and hungry, he was found and befriended by humans. Grateful for their kindness, the Irish Terrier swore he would never leave his newfound friends, and would forever guard and protect them, especially their little ones.

Kerry Blue Terrier

The Kerry Blue Terrier was developed in the rugged, mountainous area of County Kerry, Ireland, which gave him his name. Though his history is uncertain, the breed is known to have been purebred in that region for over a hundred years.

The hardworking Kerry Blue has been used to hunt on land and water, to guard homes and farms, to kill rodents, and even to herd and drive sheep and cattle. He has also been used in England as a police dog, for trailing and guarding.

The Blue in his name comes from the color of his soft and silky coat. He is born black. His coat changes gradually over the first 18 months before reaching its final blue-gray color. He requires a twice-weekly brushing and a professional scissors-trim every few months.

FUN FACTS

The Kerry Blue Terrier is renowned for his "ring presence"—that quality beyond his appearance that makes him a Kerry Blue. Judges look for a "'devil come forward'" attitude, controlled, alert, and "possessing a high pitch of beauty and an abundance of courageous vitality" (from *The Complete Kerry Blue Terrier* by E.S. Montgomery, published in 1950 by Denlinger's).

EXCERPTS FROM THE STANDARD

General Appearance:
Upstanding, balanced, with well-developed muscles.

Size, Proportion, and Substance:
Height—18½ inches at the withers; slightly smaller for females. Weight—33 to 40 pounds, with females being lighter.

IRELAND

The Lakeland Terrier is frisky, feisty, and fun. He is a smart little dog who loves to be the center of his owner's life. A person who understands this vivacious personality can have a lot of fun with a Lakeland. He's got the energy and interest to play with kids tirelessly.

If the Lakeland seems to have a lot of determination, that's because he comes from a long history of hardworking dogs. Even before fox hunting was a sport, farmers had to deal with foxes stealing their chickens. Farmers often gathered their hounds together with a group of Lakelands to hunt down their clever enemy.

Lakeland puppies are usually born dark and lighten to wheaten, red, blue, black, or liver. Sometimes the hair has black tips, and sometimes the dog has a black "saddle" over his neck, back, sides, and tail. The double coat needs brushing twice weekly and shaping every few months.

ENGLAND

FUN FACTS

The Lakeland Terrier originated in the beautiful northern area of England known as the Lake District. This is where Beatrix Potter set her stories of Peter Rabbit and other animals. Some of her books feature terriers as characters. These include *The Tale of Samuel Whiskers* and *The Tale of Ginger and Pickle*.

EXCERPTS FROM THE STANDARD

General Appearance:
Sturdily built and narrow; self-confident; alert and ready to go.

Size, Proportion, and Substance:
Height—males, 14 1/2 inches at the withers; females, about an inch shorter than males. Weight—males, 17 pounds; females slightly less.

Manchester Terrier

The sleek, tidy Manchester Terrier is the picture of elegance in a small dog. The breed is the result of crossing a descendant of the tough Black-and-Tan Terrier, a breed in England generations ago, with the graceful Whippet and Greyhound. The new dog was able to take part in two "sports" that were popular in Manchester, England, many years ago: rat killing in a pit and racing after rabbits. It was in this area that the dog was developed.

This dog has a quick, protective nature. He's happiest with gentle kids, and can be shy with new people. But he's very much a part of his own family; he attaches himself deeply to them.

The Manchester Terrier is a good friend to housekeepers because his short, glossy coat stays neat with a quick brushing once a week. There are two varieties of Manchester, the Standard and the Toy (see p. 160). They differ by size and by their ears only.

EXCERPTS FROM THE STANDARD

General Appearance:
Sleek, sturdy, elegant; bright, alert; powerful and agile.

Size, Proportion, and Substance:
Weight—12 to 22 pounds. Height— slightly less than length.

ENGLAND

Manchester Terriers have distinct markings on their coats. There is little variation. Colors must be black with rich, mohagany tan markings. The perfect tan markings are a small spot over each eye and on each cheek (called kiss marks); the entire muzzle; under the neck forming a V; part of the inside of the ears; one spot on the chest above each front leg ("rosettes"); inside the back legs; and under the tail. The rest of the dog should be black, including a black "thumb print" patch on the front of each foreleg, and a thin black line ("pencil mark") on the top of each toe.

ENGLAND

EXCERPTS FROM THE STANDARD

General Appearance:
Strongly built, active, determined, full of
fire, but having an even temper.

Size, Proportion, and Substance:
Height—10 to 14 inches at the withers.

FUN FACTS

Early in the Bull Terrier's history,
breeders thought he wasn't big
enough, so they added some
Spanish Pointer to the breed. The
resulting puppies did grow to a
larger size, but not every one of
them. There were dogs of differing
sizes. Some were so small that
they only weighed four pounds
when grown up.

Because of the variety in sizes,
breeders began to separate the
Bull Terriers into groups: Miniature (midsize), and Standard (the
largest).

The Miniature Bull Terrier is in every way—except size—exactly like the Bull Terrier. Created from crossing a Bulldog with the now-extinct White English Terrier, Bull Terriers were meant at first to be rough, tough fighting dogs. That quality never spoiled their love of people, though.

The Mini Bull is a little bundle of strength. He needs a firm, confident owner who's consistent in enforcing the rules.

His owner should have a sense of humor and playfulness, too, because the Mini Bull is full of fun. He likes to be wherever his owner is, and he's a pal to most people he meets. He proudly looks out from spitfire-black eyes that are deeply set into the distinctive egg-shaped head. His nose is black, his neck thick and muscular. His colors are solid white or colored, with any color predominating.

Miniature Schnauzer

The Miniature Schnauzer is a sweet, proud dog who loves to be the center of the household. He is devoted and playful. His special dignity shows in his whiskered face. He gets along well with people and other animals.

This German breed was created in the late nineteenth century by mixing small Standard Schnauzers with Affenpinschers and Poodles. The versatile Miniature Schnauzer has a full supply of energy, and enjoys plenty of exercise. Although he's a small dog, he is not delicate. He makes a sturdy playmate for kids, and is an excellent watchdog, too.

The Miniature Schnauzer's salt-and-pepper or black coat requires regular professional grooming. The double coat—a hard, wiry outer coat with a velvety soft undercoat—needs professional attention every few months.

EXCERPTS FROM THE STANDARD

General Appearance:
Active, alert, strong, resembling his larger cousin, the Standard Schnauzer, in general appearance.

Size, Proportion, and Substance:
Height—12 to 14 inches at the withers.

FUN FACTS

While Schnauzers were originally rat catchers, they do not share bloodlines or even country of origin with most of the other terriers. Most terriers come from Great Britain, but Miniature Schnauzers were developed in Germany. The Australian Terrier is the other terrier not from Great Britain.

GERMANY

Norfolk Terrier

The Norfolk Terrier and the Norwich Terrier were once considered the same breed. When breeders disagreed about whether the dog should have prick ears or drop ears, they decided to have two breeds: those with drop ears became the Norfolk Terrier.

Norfolks are known for their spunky, sparky personalities. They may be small, but they have endless energy and love to romp and play with children. They are outgoing and inquisitive. Being part of the family makes them happiest, and they get along nicely with all family members, including other dogs. Their wiry coats can be red, black and tan, wheaten or grizzle (grayish).

FUN FACTS

Though most Norfolks today are companions for people, they are natural rodent and vermin hunters. They fearlessly go after foxes, rabbits, and rats, not caring if they're the smaller one. They learn these skills from their mothers, who carefully and patiently teach them what to do.

ENGLAND

Norwich Terrier

The Norwich Terrier developed in England in the late nineteenth century from a variety of working terriers. He was valued for his small size—just right for riding in a basket alongside his fox-hunting master on horseback.

After the Foxhounds had forced the fox underground, the terriers would be lifted out of the baskets by their docked tails and sent after the fox. The terriers had to be courageous and feisty against the fox.

Quick, sharp, and ever-moving, the Norwich loves his daily exercise. He likes to be in the thick of the action. What is happening, who is here, where everybody's going—these are the concerns of the Norwich. Fond of children, the Norwich makes a loyal, affectionate companion.

The Norwich Terrier's coat is double—a hard and wiry outer coat in all shades of red, wheaten, black and tan grizzle, with a softer, lighter-colored undercoat. He should be brushed once or twice a week for neatness, but never clipped or shaped.

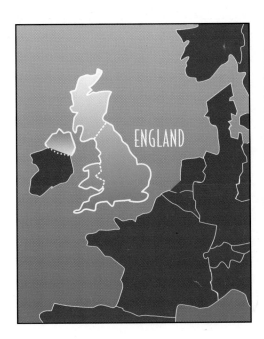

ENGLAND

FUN FACTS

"Rags" was a Norwich Terrier who lived at the end of the nineteenth century. His rough, natural, sand-colored coat was the cause for his name. He became the dog that breeders tried to copy for the perfect Norwich Terrier. This uncombed look remains part of the appeal of the breed.

EXCERPTS FROM THE STANDARD

General Appearance:
Spirited and stocky, with a foxy expression; eager and hardy.

Size, Proportion, and Substance:
Height—not more than 10 inches at withers. Weight—approximately 12 pounds.

Scottish Terrier

The Scottish Terrier is one of the oldest terriers. With his heavy whiskers and eyebrows and short body, he's instantly recognizable.

The Scottie is a playful puppy who grows into a dignified adult. He is likely to become attached to one person and lead a life of quiet dignity dedicated to that companion. Despite his sometimes reserved nature, the Scottie remains a true terrier. He wants to rid the world of rats and other vermin. He started out in Scotland as a fierce hunter of foxes and badgers. He pursued them courageously, digging into the ground after them with his broad, strong feet. The Scottie has a wiry outer coat with a shorter undercoat. He can be gray, brindled, or grizzled, black, sandy, or wheaten. His nose should be black; eyes, dark brown or nearly black.

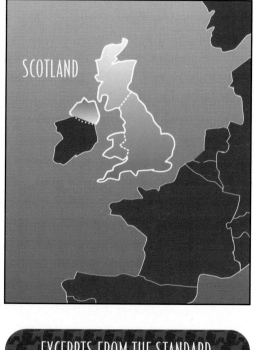

SCOTLAND

EXCERPTS FROM THE STANDARD

General Appearance:
Wearing a keen, sharp, and active expression, with head and tail carried well up, and showing power.

Size, Proportion, and Substance:
Height—about 10 inches at the withers. Weight—males, 19 to 22 pounds; females, 18 to 21 pounds.

FUN FACTS

The serious-minded Scottie often develops a deeply loving relationship with his owner. President Franklin D. Roosevelt was attached to his Scottie, Fala, who lived in the White House with Roosevelt. He took her with him on his travels whenever he could, and she is buried next to his grave in Hyde Park, New York.

The Sealyham Terrier packs as much spunk and substance in a little terrier body as you're ever likely to find, while still being a graceful and friendly dog. Sealyhams like to be around people, and have a charming sense of humor. They are able performers in obedience training, often putting their own "spin" on tricks.

Sealyhams are quiet and relaxed in the house, though they do need daily walks and romps. Sealyhams also are reliable watch dogs. Their bark is surprisingly deep for such a small dog.

Originally from Wales, Sealyhams were bred to go after foxes, badgers, and otters. Sealyham was the name of the estate of Captain John Edwardes, the man most responsible for the breed as we know it today.

Sealyhams have beautiful white coats that sometimes have lemon, tan, or badger markings on the head and ears. The outer coat is hard, while the undercoat is soft and dense. Eyes are dark; nose is black.

FUN FACTS

Though they can be independent, Sealyham Terriers are known for their sense of humor. One Sealyham, Chum, was such a little ham that she liked acting out character parts for her family and their visitors. Chum could pretend to be deathly ill, writing a letter, laughing at a joke, saying her prayers, and even flirting with the family cat by putting her "arm" around the cat's "waist." As the finale to her act, Chum would sit up and clap her paws together enthusiastically.

EXCERPTS FROM THE STANDARD

General Appearance:
Powerful and determined, keen and alert.

Size, Proportion, and Substance:
Height—10 1/2 inches at withers. Weight—males, 23 to 24 pounds; females slightly less.

WALES

Skye Terrier

With his glossy, flowing coat, the Skye Terrier may look like a dog of luxury and privilege. Actually, the breed has been a hardworking rodent exterminator for some 400 years. The Skye Terrier was strengthened by growing up in the rugged lands of Skye, a northwestern Scottish island. In this often lonely land, the Skye had no rival in exploring cairns, dens, and quarries. His famous coat protected him not only from the damp cold, but from the bite of the animals he pursued.

Skyes are devoted to their owners, but they can be serious, sensitive, and cautious around strangers. They are happiest with gentle children, and love their daily exercise.

The Skye's unusual coat must be carefully brushed out several times a week to avoid uncomfortable mats. The harsh outer coat is parted down the middle of the back and covers most of the face. The undercoat is soft and short. Colors are gray, blue, silver, platinum, fawn, tan, cream, or black. Regular trimming is necessary to keep the coat from dragging on the ground.

FUN FACTS

The most famous Skye Terrier was Greyfriar's Bobby. He belonged to a poor Scottish shepherd. When the shepherd died, the dog so loved him that he slept on the shepherd's grave every night. He guarded it for ten years, until his own death. A statue in Edinburgh commemorates his loyalty.

SCOTLAND

Soft Coated Wheaten Terrier

One of the largest terriers, though still only a medium-sized dog, the Soft Coated Wheaten Terrier is an alert and steady companion. He combines a happy outlook with a courageous spirit.

The breed has been known in Ireland for more than 200 years, and is possibly the forerunner of the Kerry Blue Terrier. Over that time he served as a herding and guarding dog and undertook the typical terrier duties of rat control.

The Soft Coated Wheaten Terrier enjoys games, especially with children. Most take pleasure in meeting strangers, whether people or other animals. He will greet friends with great joy, and loves to go places with the family. The Wheaten is a quick learner, with a steady mind, and likes plenty of exercise every day.

His soft and wavy wheat-colored coat makes him unique among all terriers. It is a single coat that grows longer on his chin and over his eyes, giving him a scruffy, working appearance.

EXCERPTS FROM THE STANDARD

General Appearance:
A medium-sized, hardy, squarish sporting terrier, with a soft, silky, gently waving coat of warm wheaten color; possessing a steady disposition; alert and happy.

Size, Proportion, and Substance:
Height—males 18 to 19 inches at the withers; females, 17 to 18 inches. Weight—males, 35 to 40 pounds; females, 30 to 35 pounds.

FUN FACTS

The Soft Coated Wheaten Terrier puppy is born with a black coat. The coat stays dark and straight the first year. In the second year it becomes very light, and doesn't yet have waves. After two years, it begins to have just the right color and waviness. The color should be wheaten—the shade of wheat ripening in a sunny field. He has brown eyes and a black nose.

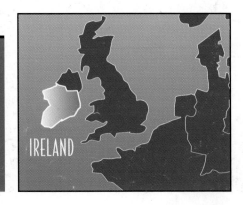

IRELAND

Early in the history of dogfighting (a cruel sport that is now illegal), big dogs such as the Mastiff and the Bulldog were the stars. But by the nineteenth century, coal miners in Staffordshire, England, wanted a smaller, faster dog. They combined the Bulldog with a small local terrier similar to the Manchester Terrier. The result was the Staffordshire Bull Terrier that we know today.

The Staffordshire Bull Terrier is a dog of high intelligence, lean muscle, and great courage. He looks forward to daily exercise, and his powerful jaws enjoy a supply of sturdy chew toys. While he is a sweet-tempered, affectionate dog, his strength and determination require an experienced owner who can work with him in a firm, but gentle, way.

The Staffie's coat is short and smooth, and needs only a quick brushing once a week. His colors are solid red, fawn, white, black, blue, or brindle.

FUN FACTS

Fighting between dogs used to be considered a sport, suitable for gambling and entertainment. Now it's against the law. Some of the breeds that were developed for the cruel sport are still around, and luckily, they've found positive ways to change with the times. The Staffordshire Bull Terrier, American Staffordshire Terrier, Bull Terrier, and Miniature Bull Terrier breeds are all living proof that fighters can also be lovers.

EXCERPTS FROM THE STANDARD

General Appearance:
A smooth-coated dog, with great strength for his size; active and agile.

Size, Proportion, and Substance:
Height—14 to 16 inches at the withers.
Weight—males, 28 to 38 pounds;
females, 24 to 34 pounds.

ENGLAND

The Welsh Terrier is a zippy little companion, always looking for action and entertainment. He loves to splash in the water and go for long country runs. Welsh Terriers are lovable buddies, and unlike some other terriers, are surprisingly well mannered with other dogs.

The Welsh Terrier fits the description of the early Welsh or Old English Wire Haired Black and Tan Terrier. The Welsh Terrier hunted otter and badger, and rode along in fox hunts to chase foxes out of their holes. His coat is always black and tan. His bushy facial hair should be combed twice a week.

FUN FACTS

The Welsh Terrier is similar in looks to his cousin the Lakeland Terrier, though slightly stockier, and to the Airedale, though the Welsh is smaller. He developed in Wales, while the Airedale and the Lakeland are from different parts of England.

EXCERPTS FROM THE STANDARD

General Appearance:
Sturdy, compact, rugged, friendly, outgoing, spirited, intelligent, and courageous.

Size, Proportion, and Substance:
Height—males, about 15 inches at the withers; females are smaller. Weight—approximately 20 pounds. Length is approximately equal to height for a square appearance.

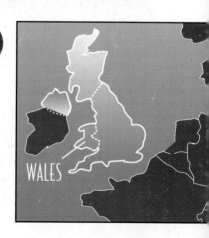

WALES

West Highland White Terrier

W ith his bristly white face and dark sparkling eyes, the West Highland White Terrier makes a smart, proud, spunky, and hearty companion. Outdoors he is a speedy and skillful hunter; indoors he is an affectionate and devoted companion. Owners will especially appreciate a typical Westie mischievousness.

The Westie loves people. His carrot-shaped tail is usually wagging, in hopes of making a new friend. With other animals he is generally friendly, but can get scrappy if not supervised. He's smart enough to learn exactly what you teach him, but he's independent enough to try a few things on his own. He will alert his family to visitors.

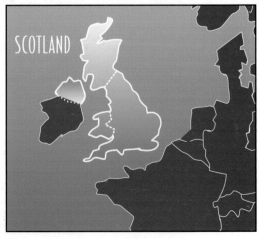

SCOTLAND

The Westie is one of the Scottish breeds of terriers. His two-inch outer coat is straight and harsh to the touch. It is a little shorter on the neck and shoulders. He needs professional clipping every few months.

 FUN FACTS

Over a hundred years ago, Cairn Terriers had litters that often included Cairns, Scotties, and Westies. The white puppies were considered unsuited to the vermin-catching work that the heather-colored Cairns performed. Breeders felt the white dogs would stand out in the scrubby landscape, then the foxes, badgers, and other vermin would be able to see the dogs and escape from them.

The Malcolms of Poltalloch, Scotland, disagreed. They preferred the little white dogs, and the family continued to breed them for many generations. They provided the ancestors for many of today's Westies.

EXCERPTS FROM THE STANDARD

General Appearance:
Strong, confident, active.

Size, Proportion, and Substance:
Height—males, 11 inches at the withers; females, 10 inches. Slightly shorter in length than in height.

TOY DOGS

There are small dogs in most of the groups, but the dogs in the Toy Group are the smallest. With their baby size and charming expressions, they are appealing to everybody. Because of their small size, though, toy breeds are delicate. Children must handle them carefully and gently. These dogs also need to be protected from hot or cold weather. The toy breeds enjoy being spoiled and petted, but not to excess. Many have big-dog personalities in their tiny-dog bodies. They don't require much living space, and will thrive in a calm family. Their size makes them portable, so you can take them almost anywhere with you.

The Toy breeds are:

Affenpinscher

Brussels Griffon

Cavalier King Charles Spaniel

Chihuahua

Chinese Crested

English Toy Spaniel

Italian Greyhound

Japanese Chin

Maltese

Manchester Terrier (Toy)

Miniature Pinscher

Papillon

Pekingese

Pomeranian

Poodle (Toy)

Pug

Shih Tzu

Silky Terrier

Yorkshire Terrier

Affenpinscher

This peppy dog has the face and impish nature of a monkey. After all, *Affenpinscher* in German means "monkey-terrier." He acts like a bigger dog as he proudly struts around.

Affenpinschers have fun-loving, sometimes mischievous, personalities. Because of their need for protection and their strong personalities, Affenpinschers become deeply attached to their family. They prefer quieter kids. When it comes to most other animals, Affenpinschers get along fine, but if threatened by another dog, the Affenpinscher can be fierce.

The Affenpinscher originated in central Europe, probably in the 1600s. He was one of several types of small terriers that moved from the barn where they caught rats, to the house, where they became beloved companions who also caught mice.

The Affenpinscher's wiry coat should be brushed and combed twice a week and trimmed twice a year. His color, usually black, can also be gray, silver, red, or black and tan.

GERMANY/ CENTRAL EUROPE

FUN FACTS

Most Affenpinschers were found around the area of Munich, Germany. But many were also found in France. There his nickname is "little devil with a moustache."

EXCERPTS FROM THE STANDARD

General Appearance:
A little, wiry-haired terrier-like toy dog whose intelligence, appearance, and attitude make him a good house pet.

Size, Proportion, and Substance:
Height—9 to 11 ½ inches at the withers. Length of the body is approximately the same as the height. Females may be slightly longer.

The Brussels Griffon is known for the almost human expression on his face. He is highly intelligent and sensitive. Even though he requires the protections needed by any toy breed, the Brussels Griffon is a total companion, bright and alert. If he feels threatened, he kicks up a big fuss.

The Brussels Griffon was developed in Belgium. He resulted from combining the Affenpinscher with a Belgian street dog—a dog similar to the Fox Terrier, except heavier. As time went on, other dogs were added to the breed. These included the Pug and the Ruby Spaniel.

The thickset Brussels Griffon can have either a rough or smooth coat. Each coat needs twice-weekly brushing and shaping every three months. Colors are red, belge (black and reddish brown mixed, usually with black mask and whiskers), black and tan, or black.

EXCERPTS FROM THE STANDARD

General Appearance:
Alert, sturdy, with a thickset, short body and expressive face.

Size, Proportion, and Substance:
Weight—8 to 10 pounds; not to exceed 12 pounds.

FUN FACTS

Early in their history, Brussels Griffons were often kept in stables as rat catchers. Gradually they became regular members of most Belgian households. Old folk songs and tales of the period mention "bearded dogs" in reference to the spunky Brussels Griffon.

BELGIUM

Cavalier King Charles Spaniel

The Cavalier King Charles Spaniel has the adoring, energetic soul of a big spaniel. But the pint-sized Cavalier, bred down from larger sporting spaniels, doesn't have the same need for large spaces. From the beginning of his history, this gentle little dog was the companion of English royalty and lived the easy life.

The Cavalier would like to be constantly by the side of his owner. He plays very happily with children, but gently. The Cavaliers does need regular exercise for good health and happiness.

The Cavalier's face has a soft, gentle expression. His eyes are large and dark. His coat is medium-long and silky. There is feathery, longer hair on his ears, chest, legs, and plume-like tail. Coat colors may be Blenheim (chestnut red and white), tricolor (black and white with tan), ruby (a rich, solid reddish brown), or black and tan (black with tan markings).

ENGLAND

EXCERPTS FROM THE STANDARD

General Appearance:
Active, graceful; fearless and happy; gentle and affectionate; elegant.

Size, Proportion, and Substance:
Height—12 to 13 inches at the withers. Weight—13 to 18 pounds.

FUN FACTS

In the seventeenth century, a "cavalier" was a knight who rode on horseback and who was loyal to King Charles I and Charles II of England. The cavaliers were considered the top of the order of knights. The cavaliers, the royal families and noblemen throughout England and France loved these little spaniels, who were named after King Charles II. They were considered house pets and appear in numerous paintings of their day.

Chihuahua

The Chihuahua is more than small; he's tiny. His adorable, apple-shaped head and big moist eyes make him nearly irresistible to kids. This sassy charmer is a healthy dog, but he is fragile. He likes to bark and scamper around, but is mainly an indoor dog, not able to tolerate cold weather.

Chihuahuas become extremely devoted to their owners, enjoying a lap-perch view on social occasions. They are also smart and high-spirited, and usually don't need much obedience training. They *do* need house-training and socializing, so it's a good idea to set up rules for acceptable behavior. This gives Chihuahuas a sense of security.

The Chihuahua's main ancestor was probably the Techichi, who existed as early as the ninth century as a favorite dog of Central American Indians. Chihuahuas appear in numerous stone carvings, and mummies of them have been found in ancient burial sites. Somewhere in their history, the Mexican hairless dog, which originally came from Asia, was bred with the smaller Techichi. Chihuahuas can have smooth or long coats. Any color—solid, marked, or splashed—is acceptable.

FUN FACTS

Much folklore surrounds the Chihuahua breed. The ancient Aztec culture of Central America may have used the dogs for religious sacrifice, burying them with their dead masters so the person's sins could be transferred to the dog. Some people believe the Chihuahua's small warm body can be used to relieve stomach upset and arthritis, or to discourage asthma attacks! True or not, the stories show the Chihuahua has long been a cherished companion.

EXCERPTS FROM THE STANDARD

General Appearance:
A graceful, alert, quick little dog with a saucy expression.

Size, Proportion, and Substance:
Not to exceed 6 pounds.

MEXICO

Chinese Crested

This exotic little dog's looks will certainly turn heads. He comes in two varieties, Hairless and Powderpuff. The Hairless is the more unusual looking of the two. He is not completely hairless. He has a tuft on his head, called his "crest," a "plume" on his tail, and his feet are covered with hair, called his "socks." All of this hair is soft, silky, and flowing. The skin should be soft to the touch, but may sometimes need moisturizing lotion. Outside, he needs lotion to keep him from getting sunburned.

The Powderpuff is covered completely with the soft, silky hair. It is a double coat—long, thin hairs lie over the softer undercoat—and needs brushing every day. Powderpuffs can be any color.

The Chinese Crested originated in Africa, but is associated with China. Chinese sailors probably brought the ancestors of today's dogs home. In China, they were bred for smallness. They became regulars on sailing boats, and were able rat killers.

These dogs are loving animals, alert and curious with plenty of energy.

CHINA

FUN FACTS

One of the people who contributed to the early popularity of this exotic-looking breed in the United States was the vaudeville performer Gypsy Rose Lee. She got her first Hairless from her sister in the 1950s and became a lifelong fan of the breed.

EXCERPTS FROM THE STANDARD

General Appearance:
Fine-boned, elegant, and graceful; loving, playful.

Size, Proportion, and Substance:
Height—ideally 11 to 13 inches at the withers.

ENGLAND

Mary, Queen of Scots, had few devoted friends at the time of her death in 1587. Among them was her English Toy Spaniel, who remained with Mary to the end, hiding inside her wide skirts until the moment of her execution. After her death, he refused to eat, and died of a broken heart.

Most dogs won't have their loyalty put to the test like Mary's dog, but this story illustrates the depth of feeling these dogs can have, and also shows the kind of company they have kept throughout their history—royalty. The breed appears in numerous noble portraits of the seventeenth, eighteenth, and nineteenth centuries. They originated in the Far East; spaniels were mixed into the breed later.

The English Toy Spaniel's coat flows like a royal cloak. It is long and silky, with extra fringe on the ears. The breed is divided into four varieties based on color: Blenheim (rich mahogany red and white); ruby (rich mahogany red); Prince Charles (white with black and tan markings); and King Charles (black and tan). The coats in the Prince Charles and King Charles varieties are longer. All need twice-weekly combing and brushing.

EXCERPTS FROM THE STANDARD

General Appearance:
A compact, square-bodied toy dog with a short nose, domed head, and merry and affectionate personality.

Size, Proportion, and Substance:
Weight—8 to 14 pounds.

FUN FACTS

One variety of English Toy Spaniel is called the King Charles. This refers to his color, black and tan; his breed is still the English Toy Spaniel. Calling him by his variety name could cause confusion with his cousin, the Cavalier King Charles Spaniel. They are two different breeds of toy spaniels. The most obvious difference is in their head shape. The English Toy has a shortened, pug-like nose, prominent eyes, chubby cheeks, and a rounder head. The Cavalier King Charles Spaniel looks more like a standard-sized spaniel, except, of course, much smaller.

Italian Greyhound

The Italian Greyhound is barely over a foot tall, but has all the grace and sweetness of his tall Greyhound relatives. He is extremely slender.

This breed is believed to be thousands of years old. Miniature Greyhounds appear in the ancient artwork of Greece and Turkey. Two-thousand-year-old skeletons of the dogs have been found by archaeologists. The dogs reached Europe by the Middle Ages. During the Renaissance, Italian noblemen adopted the breed as their own, and it became known as the Italian Greyhound.

The IG is a sporty little dog. He prances lightly in play and keeps his sense of fun throughout his life, preferring to spend most of his time with his owner. He likes attention and affection, and is a peaceful, gentle friend.

The Italian Greyhound's coat is short and smooth as satin. Because he has no undercoat, he needs the protection of a jacket in winter. He can be any color except brindle and classic black and tan.

FUN FACTS

An Italian Greyhound is not the same as a Whippet, though both dogs are small versions of the Greyhound. The Italian Greyhound is at least one-third smaller than the Whippet. He is a slimmer and more delicate dog. They both love laps, but only the Italian Greyhound was bred especially to be in one.

EXCERPTS FROM THE STANDARD

General Appearance:
Similar to the Greyhound, but much smaller and more slender; an ideal of elegance and grace.

Size, Proportion, and Substance:
Height—13 to 15 inches at the withers.

ITALY

Japanese Chin

This delightful little dog has been in the company of kings, queens, and emperors for so long now he may believe he is one of them. Though they first came from China, Japanese Chin have been the royal dog of Japan for centuries. They are proud and enjoy being pampered, though they don't become too demanding because they like people so much.

The Japanese Chin is bright and alert and likes being clean and tidy. He is playful. Sometimes he'll even make up his own tricks to show off to his audience of friends.

There is quite a bit of variety in Japanese Chin size and coat length. Most are white with black markings. They can also be white and red; the clearer and brighter the red, the better. Nose color should match the color of the markings. Eyes should be large and dark, with an eager expression. Coats should be silky and flowing, requiring twice-weekly brushing.

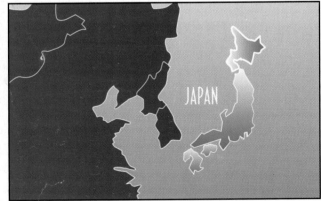

JAPAN

FUN FACTS

These little dogs lived in the Imperial Palace of Japan and were given as gifts of honor to important foreign guests. European royalty fell in love with them as well, and their popularity grew worldwide. Some people used to call them Japanese Spaniels or Chin Chin, but in 1977 the name officially became the Japanese Chin.

EXCERPTS FROM THE STANDARD

General Appearance:
Lively and dainty, with a profuse coat, stylish in movement, lifting the feet high.

Size, Proportion, and Substance:
In showing, Chin are sometimes divided into two classes, under 7 pounds and over 7 pounds.

Maltese

ITALY

EXCERPTS FROM THE STANDARD

General Appearance:
A gentle, eager, affectionate toy
dog covered with long,
silky white hair.

Size, Proportion, and Substance:
Weight—under 7 pounds; between
4 and 6 pounds preferred.

Maltese have lived luxurious lives for more than two thousand years. They are probably descended from spaniel-type dogs. They originated in Malta, an island near Italy in the Mediterranean Sea.

The Maltese becomes attached to the whole family and enjoys the company of well-behaved visitors, as well as other animals. He's got a lot of sparkle in his personality. He likes to be treated like the adorable baby of the family, but will happily respect commonsense rules.

The Maltese is a solid white cloud of silk. His fine coat should be treated like human hair—brushed every day and washed regularly. The length should be trimmed so it won't drag on the ground. He has round, dark eyes and a plume of a tail that curves over his back.

FUN FACTS

In the days when women wore long, full dresses with huge sleeves, they often tucked a tiny dog friend somewhere in the folds of their clothing. Sleeves were a favorite place to carry them, and Maltese were one of the most popular "sleeve" dogs, from the time of Queen Elizabeth I onward. In 1607, Maltese dogs were said to be the size of ferrets, another popular pet then and now.

Toy Dogs   **159**

Manchester Terrier (Toy)

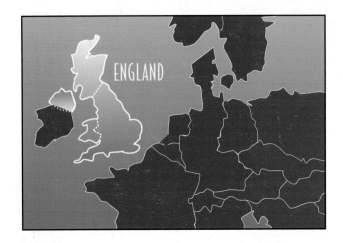

ENGLAND

EXCERPTS FROM THE STANDARD

General Appearance:
The Toy is a small version of the Standard Manchester Terrier, a small, black, short-coated dog, sleek, sturdy, yet elegant.

Size, Proportion, and Substance:
Not exceeding 12 pounds.

The Toy Manchester Terrier is a little dog with a terrier's nature. He's not the type to lounge around in laps. He'll happily charge around looking for activities and play. Gentle, consistent obedience training is good for his well-being and self-confidence. He can be shy around strangers.

The Toy Manchester Terrier is clearly descended from the original English Black and Tan Terriers. Coal miners in Manchester, England, wanted a dog for rat killing and rabbit chasing—two popular sports—so they bred the terrier with the Whippet to create the Manchester Terrier. Eventually a specific toy variety was established.

Like the Standard Manchester the Toy Manchester is glossy black with mahogany tan markings in various places over his body, including a small tan spot over each eye and one tan "kiss mark" on each cheek. No white, or any color other than black and tan, is allowed.

FUN FACTS

The Toy Manchester Terrier is a separate variety, but not a different breed, than the Standard Manchester Terrier. Toys should resemble Standards in all ways except for size and ears. Toys' ears should stand up naturally. Cropped or folded ears are not allowed.

Miniature Pinscher

A Miniature Pinscher can really spice up a person's life. This dog is small, but don't tell him—he doesn't know it. He's quick and active, with a lively curiosity, and feels he's quite important. He thoughtfully looks out for his family, bravely challenging intruders with his bold, insistent bark.

The Min Pin will be happiest with a family that treats him like a standard-sized dog. He may be stubborn, but he's also smart.

Germany is the Min Pin's country of origin. With his black and rust coloring, cropped ears, and docked tail, he does resemble his cousin the Doberman Pinscher. But he is not a miniature Dobie. *Pinscher* in German just means " terrier."

His short, glossy coat requires minimal care. Colors are red, stag red (red with black hairs), black with rust markings, or chocolate with tan.

EXCERPTS FROM THE STANDARD

General Appearance:
A sturdy, compact, smooth-coated dog, proud and alert, spirited and fearless.

Size, Proportion, and Substance:
Height—10 to 12 1/2 inches at the withers.

FUN FACTS

A distinctive feature of the Miniature Pinscher is his gait, or the way he moves. He is supposed to move with a "hackney-like action," similar to Hackney ponies. This is a high-stepping movement with a definite bend at the wrist when the foot comes up. Watch him when he moves!

GERMANY

Papillon

Papillon means "butterfly" in French. That's the name of this little dog because his wing-like ears resemble a beautiful butterfly.

But he's not likely to fly away. He prefers to cuddle with his owner, to whom he becomes affectionately attached for life. He likes to play with toys inside and is a hardy outdoor sport—perfect for city and country dwellers alike. The Papillon is highly trainable.

Papillons beautified royal laps throughout Europe for centuries. They began in Spain as miniature spaniels, and had regular drop ears then. No one knows exactly when, but by the time they reached France, some began to have upright ears. The French then called the dog the "Papillon." Papillons are mostly white with patches of other colors, usually black. Their coats are long and silky. The hair flows extra long on ears, chest and plume-like tail.

EXCERPTS FROM THE STANDARD

General Appearance:
Friendly, elegant, fine-boned, lively; different from other breeds because of his beautiful butterfly-like ears.

Size, Proportion, and Substance:
Height—8 to 11 inches at withers.

FUN FACTS

Today's Papillon is descended from the dwarf spaniel, an extremely popular toy dog of six-teenth and seventeenth century Europe. The famous French people Madame de Pompadour, Marie Antoinette, and Louis XIV were all devoted owners, and the dog was depicted in paintings by such notable artists as Rubens, Watteau, Fragonard, and Boucher.

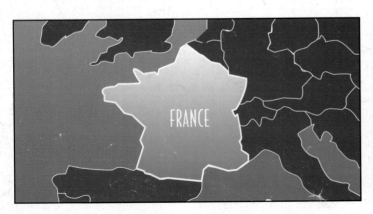

FRANCE

Pekingese

Chinese art throughout the ages abounds with images of the Pekingese, a brave but diminutive dog that has existed in China for thousands of years. The dog gets his name from the ancient city of Peking, now called Beijing. Chinese legend has it that the breed is the offspring of a lion and a monkey.

From the father lion, the legend goes, the little dogs received the shaggy mane, tufted paws, kind heart, and great courage. They inherited their mother monkey's dark, dancing eyes, turned up nose, and fun-loving, mischievous ways. Pekingese came to Europe as a result of war. When the British overtook the Chinese Imperial Palace in 1860, they returned home with several of the dogs.

Because of their thick undercoats, Pekes need at least an hourly brushing session per week. They can be in any color. A black face, especially around the eyes, with lines going to the ears, is especially preferred, though not required. They have big, round eyes and a short muzzle.

FUN FACTS

Pekingese were respected by the Chinese. Only royalty could own them. The punishment for stealing a Pekingese was death. For special ceremonies, the emperor would walk into a room with two Pekingese ahead of him barking to announce his presence, and two behind him, carrying the corners of his robe in their mouths.

EXCERPTS FROM THE STANDARD

General Appearance:
Resembling a lion in his courage, boldness, self-esteem, and independence; not dainty or delicate.

Size, Proportion, and Substance:
Less than 14 pounds.

CHINA

Pomeranian

Fragile as this dog may seem, the Pomeranian is descended from some of the heartiest dogs around: the sled dogs of Iceland and Lapland. His ancestors ended up in Germany, in the province of Pomerania, where they were bred down to the breed's present size. His nickname, Pom, comes from this province and also describes his resemblance to a pom-pom on a winter cap.

The Pomeranian is a little spark plug. He's lively, bold and inquisitive, too. This makes him an excellent and fearless watchdog despite his tiny size. He's smart and will respond well to consistent training. Poms are sometimes suspicious of strangers and other animals.

The Pomeranian's glorious double coat is one of his outstanding features. The outer coat is straight, long, and shiny. The soft woolly undercoat is thick. It causes the outer coat to stand up, especially around the neck. He needs only a twice-weekly brushing, with an occasional scissor trim. He has a foxy head with dark, shining eyes, a dark nose, and an alert expression.

EXCERPTS FROM THE STANDARD

General Appearance:
Short and squarish in the body ("cobby"), with an intelligent and alert expression.

Size, Proportion, and Substance:
Weight—3 to 7 pounds (4 to 5 is ideal).

ICELAND

FUN FACTS

In the nineteenth century, Pomeranians made their way to England. Queen Victoria liked hers so much that she had several, and they became popular throughout the land. When Queen Victoria was dying in 1901 (after a brief illness at age 89), she requested that her favorite Pom, Turi, be put in her bed to comfort her. She died with the dog beside her.

Poodle (Toy)

Toy Poodles are renowned in history for their cleverness in performing circus tricks. They were famous for being able to execute dances that seemed almost as if people were doing the steps. They charmed the upper classes, who enjoyed carrying and pampering them as cherished companions.

The Toy Poodle likes his exercise. He is usually shy and doesn't like sudden noises, but gets along fine with other animals. He is one of the smartest of all dogs, able to learn just about anything. For the Toy Poodle, gentle training lets him really show his talents.

Early in the breed's history, his larger ancestor's coat was clipped to allow him freer movement in the water while retrieving ducks. For warmth, the hair was left longer around the ankles and on top of the head and ears. Today coats are clipped for their stylish effect.

Poodles should be one color—that includes the coat, skin (nose, lips, eye rims), and nails. Colors range from black, brown, gray, and apricot to cream and white. All Poodles need professional scissoring or shaping every six weeks.

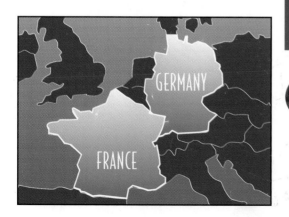

FUN FACTS

There are three sizes of Poodles—Standard, Miniature, and Toy. They are alike in every way except for size. All Poodles originated from the Standard Poodle, bred in Germany to retrieve ducks from the water. In German, *Pudel* means "water." In France, he is known as the Caniche, or duck dog. The smaller varieties were developed in France, which is why the dogs are sometimes called "French" Poodles. The tiny Toys were created especially to be companions.

EXCERPTS FROM THE STANDARD

General Appearance:
Active, intelligent, elegant, proud, carefully clipped and groomed.

Size, Proportion, and Substance:
Height—10 inches or less at the withers.

General Appearance:
A squarish, cobby dog, even-tempered, playful, charming, outgoing, and loving.

Size, Proportion, and Substance:
Weight—14 to 18 pounds.

FUN FACTS

Pugs originally had several names. In Holland they were called Mopshond, from the Dutch word "to grumble." In the early eighteenth century Marmoset monkeys were popular pets in Europe. They were known as pugs, which was a slang expression for "dear ones." With their big eyes, round faces, and impish ways, they resembled the little dogs. Soon the dogs were being called pug dogs, and the name stuck.

CHINA

When the Pug looks at you and cocks his head, even the hardest heart has to melt. And the Pug has been melting hearts for hundreds of years. Like Mastiffs, Pugs were first known in Tibet, where they were companions to Buddhist monks.

In Holland, William, Prince of Orange, was saved by his Pug in 1572. The dog, Pompey, barked and licked William's face to awaken him before an attack on his camp. Invading Spanish troops had orders to kill William. Thanks to Pompey, he survived. When William became King of England, he brought his Pugs with him. Soon the breed grew in popularity throughout Europe.

Pugs combine a cocky confidence with a friendly, sensitive nature. They are great with kids and thoroughly relish playtime and exercise.

The velvety soft coat of the Pug can be silver, apricot-fawn, or black. The silver and apricot-fawn colors should contrast sharply with his black face or mask. A black "trace" line runs down his back. His tail is tightly curled over his hip.

Shih Tzu

The Shih Tzu (SHEED-zoo) is one of the elegant, aristocratic dogs from China, cherished by royals there for over a thousand years. He is believed to have descended from a crossing of the Lhasa Apso or Tibetan Mountain Dog and the Pekingese.

American soldiers discovered the Shih Tzu in England during World War II, where the breed had been brought after the British invaded China in 1860. The Americans were charmed by the dogs and brought some home when they returned from the war.

The silky Shih Tzu is sweet and playful. He's also got plenty of spunk. He's not afraid to stand up for himself, though he usually gets along nicely with strangers and other animals. The Shih Tzu seems especially to dislike hot weather.

One big part of the Shih Tzu's life is grooming. The coat needs daily attention. It is luxurious, long, and flowing, and it must be brushed every day. All colors are allowed. His plume-like tail curls over the back.

CHINA

FUN FACTS

In the Buddhist religion, lions are important symbols of power. So the royal Chinese, practicers of Buddhism, valued little dogs that looked like the sacred lion. Shih Tzus, with their mane and proud carriage, were prized for this resemblance. In fact, the word *Shih Tzu* means "lion." Shih Tzus also have the nickname Chrysanthemum Face. The hair on their faces grows out in a circular direction, making the faces look like flowers.

EXCERPTS FROM THE STANDARD

General Appearance:
A sturdy, lively, alert toy dog with a long flowing double coat, proud, compact, and solid.

Size, Proportion, and Substance:
Height—9 to 10 1/2 inches at the withers is ideal; between 8 and 11 inches is acceptable. Weight—9 to 16 pounds.

Silky Terrier

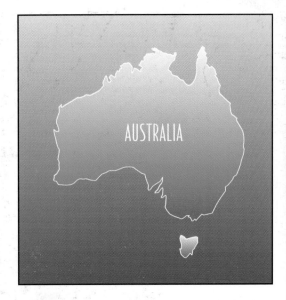

AUSTRALIA

The Silky is a spunky sprite of a dog. He is a terrier, despite the fact that he belongs to the Toy Group. He has a strong sense of himself and is eager to protect his territory.

His ancestors' original purpose was to kill rats and snakes in Australia. To make him better suited to apartment or city living, he was crossed with the tiny Yorkshire Terrier, whose coat is soft and silky. The resulting dog is the Silky Terrier—with the lustrous coat of the Yorkie, but a little larger and sportier.

The Silky is a smart dog, quick moving and quick thinking. He has an inquisitive nature and a zest for living. Obedience training is a good idea to keep him mindful of family rules.

The Silky's beautiful coat needs only a few minutes' daily grooming to keep it tangle-free. Scissoring is required every few months. The color is always the same, "blue" or silver-gray and tan. His coat is parted down the center of his back. He has dark, sparkling eyes and a black nose.

EXCERPTS FROM THE STANDARD

General Appearance:
A Toy terrier, slightly longer than tall with an inquisitive nature, full of the joy of living.

Size, Proportion, and Substance:
Height—9 to 10 inches at the withers.

FUN FACTS

During World War II, American and Canadian soldiers stationed in Australia were charmed by the Silky Terrier. They brought some Silkys back to the United States and began the interest in the breed that is now nationwide.

Yorkshire Terrier

Because they're so tiny and have such splendid coats, many people think Yorkshire Terriers are delicate dogs. Actually, it's better not to baby these dogs too much. Excessive pampering confuses them. Common sense care must be taken because of their size, but Yorkies are little terriers. That means they love to play and investigate. They are bundles of energy as puppies, though older Yorkies can be quiet and settled.

In nineteenth century Yorkshire, England, the dog caught rats for workers in clothing mills. The breed's coat was so beautiful that people said the mill workers must have spun their coats in the factories. Later in the nineteenth century, the Yorkie was discovered by high society, and he became the widely loved family companion he is today.

The Yorkie's coat is always blue and tan. The body is mostly blue, darker at the tail. The hair on the top of the head is called the "headfall." It should be a golden tan color. The tan is darker on the sides of the face, chest, and parts of legs. The Yorkie's long coat needs to be brushed every day so it won't get matted. It needs shampooing once a week and some trimming.

FUN FACTS

Yorkies are unafraid, independent, and love to travel with their people. One Yorkie took a month-long tour of the Rocky Mountains, in Colorado. She rode in a specially designed basket on a bicycle built for three (her owners and her). Of course, she had to wear her sweater on the chilly mountain mornings.

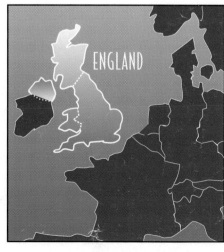

ENGLAND

EXCERPTS FROM THE STANDARD

General Appearance:
A long-haired toy terrier, vigorous and confident.

Size, Proportion, and Substance:
Weight—not to exceed 7 pounds.

Non-Sporting Dogs

This is a group for the dogs that don't especially fit any of the other categories. It's not that they don't work, it's that they're either not used for their original jobs anymore, or don't entirely conform to the qualities of another group. Regardless, the Non-Sporting breeds are companions first now. That means they like to be with their owners. Most are quick and willing learners.

There is a lot of variety in this group of individualists. Many of the breeds have colorful histories. They range in origin from the Orient (Chow Chow) to the Netherlands (Keeshond). Their former duties included coach guard (Dalmatian), good luck charm (Tibetan Terrier), and retriever (Poodle).

The Non-Sporting breeds are:

American Eskimo Dog	**French Bulldog**
Bichon Frise	**Keeshond**
Boston Terrier	**Lhasa Apso**
Bulldog	**Poodle (Standard and Miniature)**
Chinese Shar-Pei	**Schipperke**
Chow Chow	**Shiba Inu**
Dalmatian	**Tibetan Spaniel**
Finnish Spitz	**Tibetan Terrier**

American Eskimo Dog

In the early years of this century, the American Eskimo Dog was a favorite circus dog. Quick and bright in his eye-catching snowy-white coat, the Eskie was used for many acts, including one that involved walking a tightrope!

Despite what his name implies, the American Eskimo Dog is neither American nor Eskimo. In fact, he is descended from the family of European Spitz dogs, including the white German Spitz, the white Keeshond, and the white Pomeranian. His forerunner was probably brought to America in the nineteenth century by German immigrants.

Eskies come in three sizes: Toy, Miniature, and Standard, a size for every apartment and house. They are always ready for activity, and bravely announce visitors. Once introduced, they become instant friends. They have stable temperaments, and are alert and loving.

The American Eskimo Dog's snowy coat grows in a thick ruff around his neck and longer on his chest and legs. The tail is curled over and bushy. He needs twice-weekly brushing; daily when shedding. Color is solid white or white with cream. Eyes are dark to medium brown with white eyelashes.

FUN FACTS

In the early years of the American Eskimo Dog's history, circuses kept their own records, which included listings of the dogs' tricks as well as who their parents, grandparents, and other ancestors were.

EXCERPTS FROM THE STANDARD

General Appearance:
Strong and agile, alert and beautiful.

Size, Proportion, and Substance:
Height—Toy, 9 to 12 inches at withers; Miniature, over 12 inches to 15 inches; Standard, over 15 inches to 19 inches.

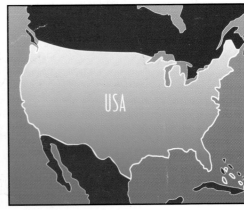

USA

Bichon Frise

MEDITERRANEAN COUNTRIES

The Bichon Frise became well known to the Italian nobility in the 1300s; in the 1500s the Bichon became a favorite of French kings and nobles, who doused him with perfume and tied ribbons into his coat. In the late 1700s the French Revolution ended the royalty, but the Bichon remained. He happily joined forces with the common people and became a companion to organ grinders as well as the blind.

This cheerful little dog looks like a gentle puffball, but is healthy and sturdy enough for play and exercise. Bichons get along with just about everyone, including strangers and other animals. They are active, alert, and curious. They are also highly trainable with gentle handling.

The Bichon's undercoat is soft and thick; the outer coat is curly and stiffer. It is trimmed evenly to show the natural outline of the dog. Hair on the ears, face, and tail is left longer. His powderpuff coat does not shed, but does require a daily brushing. He should be white with a black nose and big dark eyes.

FUN FACTS

The name Bichon Frise is pronounced BEE-shon Free-ZAY. It traces back to the dog's days as a royal French pet. He is descended from the Barbet Water Spaniel from which came the name "Barbichon" later contracted to Bichon. "Bichon Frise" is French for "fluffy little dog."

EXCERPTS FROM THE STANDARD

General Appearance:
Small, sturdy, cheerful, with a jaunty and inquisitive expression.

Size, Proportion, and Substance:
Height—9 1/2 to 11 1/2 inches at the withers is preferred; 9 to 12 inches is allowed.

Boston Terrier

The Boston Terrier—a native American breed—is known for his sunny disposition. He is happy to know you and to be your friend, and is content to live in the city or the country.

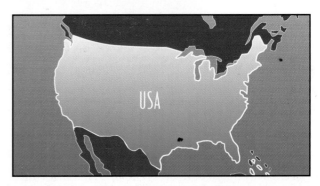

The Boston Terrier resulted from a cross between the English Bulldog and a kind of white English terrier during the late nineteenth century. For a while the breed was called Bull Terrier, but there was already a breed with that name. Since the dog was developed in Boston, he was given the name of that city. The Boston Terrier is descended from two kinds of fighting dogs, but he is a loving companion.

Boston Terriers enjoy lots of attention from their family. They get along with other pets, especially when introduced at an early age. Even though they are small, they'll bark to let their family know if someone is at the door. The Boston Terrier is a highly intelligent dog.

The Boston has white on his face, chest, front legs, and feet. The rest should be black or brindle. A quick weekly brush-through keeps his coat gleaming. In cold weather, he requires a sweater for walks or outdoor activity.

EXCERPTS FROM THE STANDARD

General appearance:
Lively, highly intelligent, with a smooth coat, short head and compact body. He expresses determination, strength, and style.

Size, Proportion, and Substance:
Weight is divided by classes: under 15 pounds, 15-20 pounds, 20-25 pounds

FUN FACTS

Dressed in his black and white "tuxedo," the Boston Terrier carries himself with great dignity. His nickname is the American Gentleman. He is one of the few breeds developed in the United States.

Bulldog

He was originally a fighting dog, but now he's about as easygoing as a dog can be. The Bulldog is intelligent and trainable, but because of his face and body type, light exercise is enough to keep him healthy, and an air-conditioned house is his favorite place in the summer.

Bulldogs are devoted to their families and get along well with other pets. They especially like kids. They normally won't bark at visitors, but in an emergency, an intruder could discover just how powerful their massive jaws are.

The Bulldog was probably created by breeding Mastiffs and terriers together. He earned the name Bulldog from a cruel sport, "bullbaiting," that involved the dog pinning a bull by its nose. Bullbaiting was outlawed in 1778.

His short coat only needs once-a-week brushing, but his face feels better with daily cleaning, especially in the wrinkles. His short, fine coat should be red brindle; all other brindles; solid white; solid red, fawn, or fallow; or Piebald, in which the color patches are well defined.

ENGLAND

EXCERPTS FROM THE STANDARD

General Appearance:
Medium-sized with a smooth coat and heavy, low-swung body, a massive short-faced head, wide shoulders, and sturdy limbs. Equally strong, courageous, and kind; peaceful and dignified.

Size, Proportion, and Substance:
Weight—males, about 50 pounds; females, about 40 pounds.

FUN FACTS

The formerly ferocious Bulldog serves as the mascot of England, of Yale University, and of the United States Marine Corps.

Chinese Shar-Pei

In 1973, a Hong Kong breeder of Chinese Shar-Peis (whose name translates from Chinese roughly as "sandpaper coat") appealed to dog lovers in an American magazine. He asked them to help save this exotic and ancient breed, which was in danger of dying out after the Chinese government nearly eliminated the country's dog population after World War II. A handful of the breed, whose history is not fully known, was exported to the United States in a successful effort to save them from extinction.

While very loving toward his family, the Shar-Pei has an independent nature. He may seem uninterested in other people around him and cautious with other animals. Because he is able to think for himself, obedience training requires a strong and patient person. This is a serious and dignified dog.

The Shar-Pei coat can be any solid color, and comes in two lengths: a short "horse" coat or a longer "brush" coat. He may share some ancestry with the Chow Chow; both dogs have blue tongues. His tail curls around. The puppy's face is much more wrinkled than the adult's.

EXCERPTS FROM THE STANDARD

General Appearance:
Active, dignified, alert, medium-sized.

Size, Proportion, and Substance:
Height—18 to 20 inches at the withers.
Weight—40 to 55 pounds.

FUN FACTS

Here in the United States, the Shar-Pei's face is described as having a "hippopotamus muzzle." In China, the descriptions of many of the dog's features are poetical: melon head, clamshell ear, butterfly nose, mother frog mouth, grandma face, water buffalo neck, shrimp back, dragon leg, garlic feet, and iron toenail.

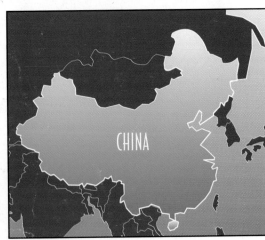

CHINA

Chow Chow

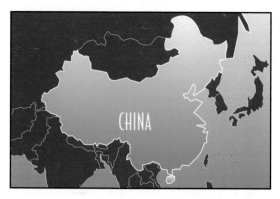

CHINA

General Appearance:
Powerful and sturdy, of Arctic type, elegant, dignified, with a scowling expression and straight-legged walk.

Size, Proportion, and Substance:
Height—17 to 20 inches at the withers.

The fuzzy, adorable Chow Chow puppy becomes a powerful and independent dog in a few short months. The Chow is highly intelligent and extremely loyal to his owner, but is for an experienced dog owner. He is serious, dignified, and proud. His history explains why.

The Chow Chow was bred in Northern China, probably at least two thousand years ago, to hunt, herd, and protect the home. His ancestors could be the Tibetan Mastiff and the Siberian Samoyed, though he may be even older than these breeds. His history is one of hard work and little "fun" with humans, so the Chow Chow may seem a little aloof.

During the 1700s, ships brought goods from China to the West. Captains had to keep lists of everything on board. Sometimes there were boxes filled with many little objects. Captains would list these with a slang word, "chow chows." It meant the same as doodads or this-and-thats. The dogs were shipped from China along with these crates of chow chows, so they became known as chow chow dogs.

Grooming is a major consideration with Chow Chows. There are two coat types for the breed: rough (long) and smooth (shorter). Both require twice-weekly brushing. Colors are reds, black, blue-cinnamon, and cream. The tail is curled. Eyes are almond-shaped and dark brown. The nose is black; the tongue is blue-black.

Dalmatian

The Dalmatian has many talents. He has been used to herd sheep, pull carts, track and retrieve, kill rats, and perform in circuses. In England, before the time of automobiles, he rose to his greatest fame as a working companion to coach drivers, owing to his happy, hard-working attitude.

The Dalmatian's origins are mysterious. While researchers know they are an ancient breed, no one can be certain exactly where they came from. That may be because they were developed over the centuries by nomadic peoples wandering throughout Europe. The dogs were given the name Dalmatian after an area in the former Yugoslavia called Dalmatia.

He is a well-behaved gentleman, but needs plenty of exercise. He loves to jog for miles alongside his owner. He is reliably polite with strangers, but also a good watchdog. His love and devotion to his owner are boundless.

Dalmatians have short, hard coats with no undercoat. They need a quick daily brushing because they shed year round. Puppies are born white and develop their spots in two to six weeks. The spots, which can be black or liver, should range in size from a dime to half-dollar.

EASTERN EUROPE

FUN FACTS

When horse-drawn carriages were the way to travel, many drivers kept Dalmatians to trot alongside the coach. Here they put many of their skills to work. If loose farm animals wandered onto the road, they would herd them out of the coach's path. And when the driver stopped for a rest and a bite to eat at the village inn, he knew he could safely leave his coach and horses under the watchful eye of his Dalmatian. The dog's steady character even gave confidence to skittish horses as they traveled. For all these reasons, the Dalmatian was prized by firefighters using horse-drawn wagons. He became renowned as their mascot.

EXCERPTS FROM THE STANDARD

General Appearance:
Poised and alert, distinctively spotted, muscular and active, not shy, intelligent.

Size, Proportion, and Substance:
Height—between 19 and 23 inches at the withers.

Finnish Spitz

This beautiful dog looks like a fox, and he's as clever as one. For hundreds of years the Finnish Spitz has helped the people of Finland hunt game birds. In fact, he is the national dog of Finland.

The Finnish Spitz belongs to the ancient Spitz dog family that can be traced back thousands of years. Huskies are the most familiar descendant. Like Huskies, Finnish Spitz dogs have pointed ears, narrow noses, dense double coats, and curled tails. Snow is their friend.

Finnish Spitz dogs are devoted to their families and love frisky play with kids. They are active and "barkative," with sounds ranging from soft "singing" and yodeling to high-pitched barking. They are intelligent, independent thinkers. While Finn's are affectionate with their families, they may be shy around strangers and other dogs.

The Finn's glorious red-gold double coat consists of a downy soft undercoat with harsher, longer hair for the outer coat. The colors range from pale honey to deep auburn. The undercoat is slightly lighter, which creates an over-all glowing appearance. He needs brushing at least twice a week; daily when shedding. Eyes are dark and almond-shaped. The nose is black.

FUN FACTS

The Finnish Spitz tracks birds by sight, sound, and scent. Once he finds a bird, he rushes up to it and scares it into a tree. Then he begins a soft yodel-like barking, and swings his tail slowly back and forth. While the bird remains hypnotized by the tail action, the dog barks louder and louder to attract the attention of the hunter. He points out the bird to the hunter by looking straight at it.

FINLAND

EXCERPTS FROM THE STANDARD

General Appearance:
A fox-like dog with pointed muzzle and erect ears; lively, quick moving, cloaked in a magnificent red coat.

Size, Proportion, and Substance:
Height—males, 17 ½ to 20 inches; females, 15 ½ to 18 inches.

French Bulldog

Looking like a small, bat-eared version of the Bulldog, the French Bulldog is a completely different dog from his English cousin. In the mid-1800s, the English developed several types of miniature Bulldogs. They never became popular in England, but in France the idea caught on. The dog that developed in France, often called the Frenchie, has a unique appearance, set off by his wide, rounded ears and dome-shaped forehead.

The French Bulldog is a mild-tempered companion dog looking for friendship with people and animals alike. Sturdy and muscular, he enjoys playing with children, but sometimes favors the company of one special person.

He's a clean dog. His short coat requires only weekly brushing. Although he is an excellent watchdog, he doesn't bark without a cause.

French Bulldogs have short, smooth, shiny coats that come in brindle (brown with black stripes), fawn, white, and brindle and white. They should not be solid black, mouse, liver, black and tan, or black and white. The "bat" ears are broad at the base, long, and have rounded tips. His nose is black.

EXCERPTS FROM THE STANDARD

General Appearance:
Active, intelligent, muscular, with a smooth coat and alert and interested expression.

Size, Proportion, and Substance:
Weight—not more than 28 pounds.

When the weather gets hot, Frenchies like to stay inside in an air conditioned setting. For all the short-faced dogs, breathing can be difficult in muggy, hot conditions. Frenchies can really feel the heat.

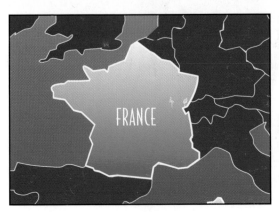

FRANCE

Keeshond

The Keeshond (KAZE-hond) is a happy dog by nature. He has always been like that. The national dog of Holland was never asked to hunt, herd, or do anything except be a friend to people. And he's very good at that job.

Keeshonden (plural for Keeshond) are extremely affectionate. When a Keeshond joins the family, he looks forward to being an important part of it. He loves children and will gladly play games and bounce around with them.

The Keeshond is descended from the arctic Spitz type. Their lush, double coat has a harsh, outer coat that stands out from the softer one underneath. It is longest on the neck, where it forms a broad mane. The tail is a fluffy plume. He is always a mixture of gray, black, and cream.

EXCERPTS FROM THE STANDARD

General Appearance:
A handsome dog attracting attention by his coat, coloring, alertness, and intelligent, foxlike expression.

Size, Proportion, and Substance:
Height—males, 17 to 19 inches at the withers; females, 16 to 18 inches.

FUN FACTS

The government leader in eighteenth century Holland, William, Prince of Orange, was often seen in public with his little Pug dog, Pompey. Opposing him politically were the Patriots, the party of the people. Their leader was Kees de Gyselaer. He had a beautiful dog, also named Kees, whose picture was used as the symbol for the Patriot Party. This dog became known as the Keeshond. The Patriots were defeated, but the Keeshond lived on to become the national dog of Holland.

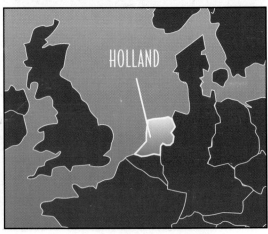

HOLLAND

Lhasa Apso

Although the Lhasa Apso may at first seem to resemble the Shih Tzu, the Lhasa is a little bigger, is groomed differently and has a different history and character. Shih Tzus were pampered by Chinese royalty; Lhasas originated and developed in the harsh, secluded Tibetan mountains, working as guards of Buddhist monasteries. Mastiffs guarded the outside walls of the monasteries. Lhasas were stationed inside, as the second line of protection. They held the job because of their keen hearing, protectiveness, and ability to know whether a visitor was a friend or a stranger.

Lhasas don't expect to be pampered. They are protective of their people and care for them in a dignified but loving manner. In obedience training, positive, repetitive lessons will win the Lhasa over. The Lhasa can be playful and spirited, but also independent.

The Lhasa is best known for his long, dense, lustrous coat. It is thick, straight, and hard, not woolly or silky. It can be any color, and it needs daily care.

EXCERPTS FROM THE STANDARD

General Appearance:
Bold and happy, but wary of strangers.

Size, Proportion, and Substance:
Height—about 10 or 11 inches at the withers; females, slightly smaller.

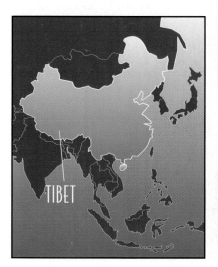

TIBET

FUN FACTS

Lhasa Apsos guarded Tibetan villages and monasteries for 800 years. The highest priest of the Buddhists, the Dalai Lama, presented Lhasas as gifts of honor to visiting emperors and other important guests. Lhasas were considered symbols of good luck.

Poodle (Standard and Miniature)

Poodles are smart, loyal, proud, and fun. The Poodles' intelligence is clear in the knowing gaze they give to all they observe. They seem to understand the moods of their special friends. They enjoy the challenges of obedience training, which gives these intelligent dogs great happiness. Politely reserved around strangers, they can also have a playful sense of humor.

EXCERPTS FROM THE STANDARD

General Appearance:
Active, intelligent, and elegant, squarely built, well-proportioned, moving soundly, and carrying himself proudly.

Size, Proportion, and Substance:
Heights—Standard, more than 15 inches at withers; Miniature, more than 10 but less than 15 inches; and Toy, 10 inches or less.

The Poodle was prized by hunters as a water retriever of birds as far back as the fifteenth and sixteenth centuries in Germany. In France Poodles were also used as retrievers and performing circus dogs. Poodles come in three types—Standard, Miniature, and Toy (see p. 165)—depending on size. Otherwise the types are identical in appearance. All are one breed, governed by the same standard.

Poodles require serious grooming. Their top coat is thick, harsh, and curly, and the undercoat is woolly and warm. The coat does not shed much, but it requires daily brushing and professional grooming once a month. All colors are solid, and can be white, black, brown, gray, blue, apricot, cream, and more. Skin color varies also: pink, cream, blue, or silver.

Miniature Poodle

FUN FACTS

Despite their glamorous looks, Poodles were originally hard-working water dogs. They were developed in Germany but may share ancestors with other similar dogs in Russia, France, and Southwestern Europe. The English word *Poodle* comes from the German *pudel* or *pudelin*, which means "to splash in the water." The coat, clipped to make swimming easy, was left longer on the head, chest, and feet for warmth.

Standard Poodle

The Schipperke's name means "little captain" in Flemish, and that well describes the personality of this peppy, confident dog. The Schipperke (SKIP-er-kee) needs to make sure everything is shipshape. He wants to know where people are and what they're up to.

The Schip has a can-do attitude. He is quick-thinking and quick-moving. He is unaware of his small size, and eagerly enters into play with dogs of any kind or size.

The Schip shares a common ancestry with the Groenendael, the large black Belgian Sheepdog. In the seventeenth century, the Schip was bred to be small because he lived in small shoe shops and on canal barges. He was used as a guard dog and ratter.

Schips are always black. Their double coat has a stand-up ruff, a "cape," and full-coated trousers. Their appearance is foxy: pointed noses and upright ears, and "cobby," meaning short-bodied. Their coat needs only a once-a-week brushing. Their tails are traditionally docked.

BELGIUM

EXCERPTS FROM THE STANDARD

General Appearance:
An agile, active watchdog and hunter of vermin, thickset and cobby, with a fox-like face.

Size, Proportion, and Substance:
Height—males, 11 to 13 inches at withers; females, 10 to 12 inches.

FUN FACTS

One beautiful Schipperke can be seen in Beatrix Potter's book *The Pie and the Patty Pan.* This Schip, Duchess, entertains her hostess by performing tricks for her and has other adventures.

Shiba Inu

Seen today throughout Japan, the Shiba Inu is a favorite Japanese companion dog. *Shiba* means "brushwood" in Japanese, and *Inu* means "dog." The Shiba began his history in the rugged mountains of Japan, where he was valued as a bold, alert, and athletic hunter, able to scramble up steep slopes and handle the terrain. His tough opponents included wild boars.

The Shiba was brought to the United States in 1954 by an American family that had lived in Japan and knew firsthand the loving qualities of this steady companion. His popularity continues to rise.

Spirited as he is outside, the Shiba is a tidy dog indoors. He often washes his face with his paws like a cat. Sometimes he jumps high in the air trying to catch birds.

Coloring and markings give the Shiba his foxy look. He can be red, red sesame, or black and tan. His deep, plush double coat needs brushing several times a week. He sheds every few months.

EXCERPTS FROM THE STANDARD

General Appearance:
A small, muscular dog; compact and well furred; alert and active.

Size, Proportion, and Substance:
Height—males, 14 1/2 to 16 1/2 inches at the withers; females, 13 1/2 to 15 1/2 inches. Males are slightly heavier than females.

JAPAN

FUN FACTS

One day in the 1970s, a woman found a reddish-brown dog on the side of a busy highway in California. Julia Caldwell brought the dog home, and her family fell in love with "Rusty." Caldwell was curious about what kind of dog he could be. She found a picture of a similar dog, a Shiba Inu, in a book. She contacted the Japanese diplomatic office in her city to verify her discovery, but they couldn't help her. So she wrote the Japanese Kennel Club, sending along a photograph of Rusty. The Japanese value this breed so highly that the Japanese Kennel Club sent a representative to the United States to examine Rusty. Rusty was declared to be a pure-bred Shiba Inu and was given official registration papers. Caldwell imported a mate for Rusty from Japan and became one of the first Shiba Inu breeders in this country.

Tibetan Spaniel

EXCERPTS FROM THE STANDARD

General Appearance:
Small, active, alert, longer in body than high.

Size, Proportion, and Substance:
Height—About 10 inches at the withers.
Weight—9 to 15 pounds.

FUN FACTS

One of the Tibetan Spaniel's favorite activities is sitting in a high spot and watching what everyone is doing. That hobby may have begun long ago, when the dog was a guard for isolated Buddhist monasteries in Tibet as well as a companion for the monks.

The Tibetan Spaniel has existed for thousands of years in Tibet and China, and holds an important position in Tibetan culture. In the Tibetan form of Buddhism, the dog is the symbol of obedience to the peaceful, loving power of Buddha. Chinese Buddhists were often buried with small statues of dogs so that they would have company in the afterlife. Animals are believed to have souls that are no different from human souls.

This dog is beloved all over the world, too. He is intelligent and loving. He's not a lap dog, even though he's small. He's a brave watchdog and likes to take walks and play. Tibetan Spaniels get along well with other animals, especially other dogs.

The Tibetan Spaniel has a glossy, silky coat with feathery hair on ears, toes, and front legs. He has a cape of longer hair over his neck and longer hair on his back legs. The double coat needs only weekly brushing except during shedding season, when five minutes a day helps keep it under control. He can be any color.

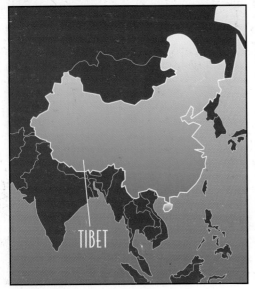

TIBET

Tibetan Terrier

The Tibetan Terrier looks like a small English Sheepdog, but he was never used for herding. He wasn't used for guarding, either. He has always been a companion dog. The Tibetan Terrier was considered a member of the family in his native Tibet, and treated as if he was one of the children. That's probably why to this day the Tibetan Terrier enjoys people so much. He is a happy, outgoing dog. Tibetan Terriers are actually not terriers. They only have that name because of their size and because Western countries preferred it to the dog's Tibetan names, Luck Bringer and Holy Dog.

Tibetan Terriers are extremely agile. They can use their paws like cats to wash, catch, hold, and even bat at tennis balls. They are usually quiet. When they do bark, the sound starts out low and rises to a high pitch.

Grooming is a consideration with this breed. He needs brushing and combing nearly every day, especially as he approaches adulthood. His hair is long and shaggy, and covers his big brown eyes. The coat may be straight or wavy. It can be any color.

FUN FACTS

The Tibetan Terrier is adaptable to snow and harsh conditions because he developed in the Lost Valley of the Tibetan mountains, an area of Tibet cut off from the rest of the world. When someone did make a visit, he was often rewarded with the gift of a Tibetan Terrier. The dog was considered good luck for the return trip. People never sold their Tibetan Terriers. They believed that could bring bad luck to the whole village.

EXCERPTS FROM THE STANDARD

General Appearance:
Medium-sized, profusely coated, powerful, with large, flat, round feet shaped like snowshoes.

Size, Proportion, and Substance:
Height—males, 15 to 16 inches; females, slightly smaller. Weight—18 to 30 pounds, but usually 20 to 24 pounds.

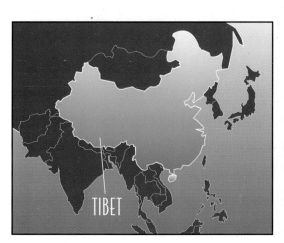

TIBET

HERDING DOGS

This group works with herds of sheep and cattle, controlling their movements. Herding dogs have been prized by shepherds and farmers for centuries. They are quick, strong, and highly intelligent. They are excellent learners and look to their owners for instructions on their behavior.

Even without training, they naturally start herding. A Herding dog can sometimes see people or pets as creatures to be herded; some may gently push or nip at heels, as they do for sheep and cattle.

Herding dogs need lots of exercise, or they can become bored and get into mischief. They need to work, even if that means playing an organized game with their owner. Some are barkers when they have something to communicate. They are extremely loyal to their families.

The Herding breeds are:

Australian Cattle Dog	**Briard**
Australian Shepherd	**Collie**
Bearded Collie	**German Shepherd Dog**
Belgian Malinois	**Old English Sheepdog**
Belgian Sheepdog	**Puli**
Belgian Tervuren	**Shetland Sheepdog**
Border Collie	**Welsh Corgi, Cardigan**
Bouvier des Flandres	**Welsh Corgi, Pembroke**

Australian Cattle Dog

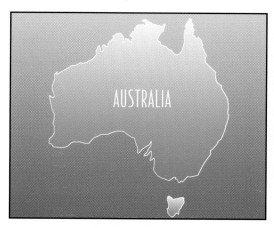

AUSTRALIA

Farmers in nineteenth century Australia needed a tough but obedient dog to help round up their cattle over hundreds of miles of fenceless land, where the climate was often harsh. The Australian Cattle Dog came into being as the result of crossing a Dingo, the wild Australian dog, with a Scottish Highland Collie. Dalmatians were also added to increase the dogs' faithful protectiveness and working ability with horses, which the farmers rode on the roundups.

Australian Cattle Dogs are hard workers today on farms throughout the world. They need to run, to chase, to herd, and to play with their owners. They are sometimes suspicious of people and dogs they don't know. They are obedient, but training takes patience because they're also independent.

The Australian Cattle Dog's coat is one of the breed's unique features. It reflects his ancestors' different coats. The breed is born white like a Dalmatian, then develops into either "blue" or "red speckle." Blues are mostly gray with black; reds are red-brown with white hairs sprinkled throughout.

FUN FACTS

In Australia there's a type of wild dog that's been there since the Stone Age, the Dingo. The Australian Cattle Dog still resembles his Dingo ancestors. The Dingo became friends with the Aborigine tribespeople. Dingos helped the people hunt game, such as kangaroos. They slept curled up with the people at night to keep them warm. A chilly Australian night is called a Three Dog Night, because people needed three dogs to keep them warm on those nights.

EXCERPTS FROM THE STANDARD

General Appearance: Sturdy, powerful, muscular, with great agility and endurance. Ever alert, intelligent, courageous, and trustworthy, with a devotion to duty.

Size, Proportion, and Substance: Height—males, 18 to 20 inches at withers; females, 17 to 19 inches.

Intelligent and very alert, the Australian Shepherd gives complete devotion to his owner. All he asks in return is the chance to work. He was bred to herd livestock, and is serious and single-minded about his job. If he sees sheep, geese, chickens, goats, ducks—even a group of children—he'll immediately start herding.

The Aussie is unhappy if he does not get enough exercise and purposeful activity. He loves to play ball, catch flying disks, and participate in obedience, agility, tracking, herding, and carting events. He's always ready to go on a hike and is happy to carry his own supplies in his pack.

The Australian Shepherd's water-resistant coat enables him to adapt to various conditions and to work long hours in foul weather. Coat color is black, blue merle, red merle, and red with or without white markings and/or tan points.

FUN FACTS

Despite its name, the Australian Shepherd did not originate in Australia. Descended from herding dogs used over 12,000 years ago, the Aussie might have evolved from several herding breeds that came to America with early settlers from Europe. Another version says the breed originated in Spain, went to Australia, then came to California during the Gold Rush of 1849.

EXCERPTS FROM THE STANDARD

General Appearance:
Confident, strong desire to work, reserved with strangers, intelligent, trainable, curious, loyal to owner.

Size, Proportion, and Substance:
Height—18 to 23 inches at the withers.
Weight—45 to 60 pounds.

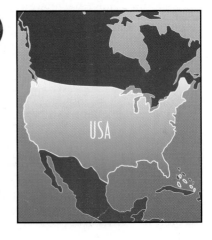

USA

Bearded Collie

This dog is one of Britain's oldest breeds. Beardies are believed to have originated with the Komondor in central Europe, but were used to herd animals in Scotland for so long that they became known as the Highland Collie. Later the name was changed to the Bearded Collie, since they have long facial hair unlike other Collies.

Bearded Collies are still actively working as herders today. But they excel as pets, too. Though best suited to suburban or country living, Beardies can be happy in the city with plenty of exercise.

Beardies are outgoing and friendly, intelligent, and have a lively sense of humor. Those qualities mean training will go better if it is not too repetitious.

Like most long-haired breeds, Bearded Collies require a commitment to grooming. They need a few minutes of brushing or combing every day.

ENGLAND

EXCERPTS FROM THE STANDARD

General Appearance:
Hardy and active, strong, devoted, and intelligent, with a bright, inquiring expression.

Size, Proportion, and Substance:
Height—males, 21 to 22 inches at withers; females, 20 to 21 inches.

FUN FACTS

Bearded Collies have been so well loved through the centuries that they have even been included in portrait paintings. One is by the famous artist Gainsborough, who in 1771 painted the Duke of Buccleigh with his Beardie. A year later, the painter Reynolds included his Beardies in a portrait of his wife and daughter.

Belgian Malinois

The Belgian Malinois (MAL-e-nwah) is one of the three breeds of Belgian sheepdogs recognized by the AKC. The other two are the Belgian Sheepdog and the Belgian Tervuren. The main differences among them are their coat lengths and colors. The Malinois gets his name from the town of Malines, Belgium, where he was developed.

The Belgian Malinois is smart and highly sensitive to his surroundings. He is a devoted companion to his family, but can be shy around strangers. He lives best around gentle children, and makes a careful watchdog. Obedience training requires firmness with the right amount of gentleness. Malinois are active dogs. They excel in herding, search and rescue, and narcotics-detection police work.

The beautiful and elegant Belgian Malinois looks like a smaller, slimmer version of the German Shepherd. He has a tan coat with a black face and upright ears. He needs brushing only once a week, except when he's shedding.

FUN FACTS

The Malinois is the Belgian dog most often used for sheep herding in Belgium. In the United States, he is one of the rarest AKC-recognized breeds, but his numbers are growing as people recognize his superior intelligence and abilities.

EXCERPTS FROM THE STANDARD

General Appearance:
Elegant and proud, agile, alert, and full of life, solid without bulkiness.

Size, Proportion, and Substance:
Height—males, 24 to 26 inches at withers; females, 22 to 24 inches.

BELGIUM

196 AKC-Recognized Breeds, by Group

Belgian Sheepdog

Of the three types of Belgian sheepdogs, only one is called the Belgian Sheepdog in this country. He is also known as the Groenendael, named for Chateau Groenendael, located near Brussels, Belgium.

This is an active, extremely loyal dog. He's happiest with an owner who can give him plenty of jobs to do (like playing games and obedience training). The Belgian Sheepdog gets along with gentle children and does best in country or suburban living with lots of exercise. He is protective of his family.

A close look at the Belgian Sheepdog shows that he and the little Schipperke probably shared a common ancestor. Both have upright ears, a fine, pointed muzzle, alert dark eyes, and a glorious, glossy black coat. The Belgian Sheepdog's coat is straight and abundant with longer hair around the neck and behind the front legs. The back legs are thickly coated in "trousers." The tail is covered with long, thick hair. He needs brushing about twice a week, daily during shedding.

FUN FACTS

Belgian Sheepdogs have proved their smarts many times over. They perform well in sports like obedience, herding, and tracking. They work as search and rescue dogs, guide dogs, and therapy dogs. Most heroically, they performed valuable services during World Wars I and II. They carried messages, pulled ambulance wagons and machine guns, and guarded military sites.

EXCERPTS FROM THE STANDARD

General Appearance:
Elegant and proud; strong, agile, alert; solid, but not bulky.

Size, Proportion, and Substance:
Height—males, 24 to 26 inches at withers; females, 22 to 24 inches.

BELGIUM

Like the other Belgian sheepdogs (the Malinois and the Belgian Sheepdog), the Belgian Tervuren (Ter-VYUR-en) is a beautiful, intelligent dog that likes challenging activities and nearly constant companionship. The Tervuren gets his name from the Belgian village of Tervuren, where the breed's herding and guarding were vital to the everyday life of the people in the farming villages. They were also loving family companions.

Tervurens excel in activities and competitions. They make top-notch therapy or guide dogs for the disabled, and of course they are excellent at their original job, herding.

The Tervuren's thick, lustrous coat is long, usually rich fawn to russet mahogany with black overlay. The underparts of the body, the tail, and the trousers are lighter—cream, gray, or light beige. The tail has a dark tip. Brushing should be done twice a week, daily during shedding seasons. The outer coat darkens as the dog matures.

FUN FACTS

The differences among the Belgian sheepdogs are in their coats. The Malinois has a short, tan coat with a black face; the Belgian Sheepdog has a long, shiny black coat; and the Tervuren has a long, multi-colored coat. All of these breeds are intelligent, sensitive, and active, with a noble history of hard work.

EXCERPTS FROM THE STANDARD

General Appearance:
Displaying intelligence, courage, alertness, and devotion.

Size, Proportion, and Substance:
Height—males, 24 to 26 inches at withers; females, 22 to 24 inches.

BELGIUM

Border Collie

The supreme sheep herding dog, the Border Collie lives to work. This is the dog for the athletic person who is ready to engage a dog in directed activities.

A Border Collie's idea of work includes driving sheep and other animals; obedience and agility competitions; search and rescue; narcotics and bomb detection; guide dog for the blind and deaf; and even movie and television actor. His intense concentration, deep desire to please, as well as speed and intelligence give the breed the edge in just about any job he undertakes.

Border Collies have been cherished by farmers for hundreds of years. They arose in the "border" area between Scotland and England.

Border Collies may have a longer (rough) coat or a shorter (smooth) coat. The rough-coated are more familiar in the United States. Most Border Collies are black with white, or black and tan with white. However, they may be any color except solid white.

SCOTLAND/ ENGLAND

EXCERPTS FROM THE STANDARD

General Appearance:
A graceful and agile medium-sized dog; energetic, alert, and eager; highly intelligent. Body is slightly longer than high.

Size, Proportion, and Substance:
Height—males, approximately 19 to 22 inches at withers; females, 18 to 21 inches.

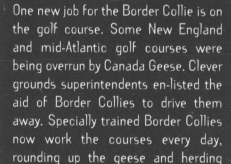

FUN FACTS

One new job for the Border Collie is on the golf course. Some New England and mid-Atlantic golf courses were being overrun by Canada Geese. Clever grounds superintendents en-listed the aid of Border Collies to drive them away. Specially trained Border Collies now work the courses every day, rounding up the geese and herding them off the grounds.

Bouvier des Flandres

The Bouvier des Flandres (BOO-vee-ay duh Flaun-druh) was originally a farm dog from the area of Flanders in Belgium. There he performed the work of herding cattle and guiding them to the marketplace. He also hauled milk and butter to town in carts. Some of his early names were Dirty Beard, Cow Dog, and Cattle Driver.

Bouviers are big and big-hearted. They are strong and can think for themselves.

The Bouvier is protective. He can sometimes be suspicious of other dogs. While he's not overly active in the house, he does need plenty of exercise. Country or suburban living suits him well.

The Bouvier's coat protects him in all sorts of weather. It has a tousled appearance—it looks like it's been blown around by the wind. His color is usually black or gray, but Bouviers can also be fawn, brindle (tan with black stripes), or salt and pepper. The tail is docked.

BELGIUM

EXCERPTS FROM THE STANDARD

General Appearance:
Powerfully built, rough-coated, and rugged. Agile, spirited, and bold, yet serene and well-behaved; intelligent, active, fearless.

Size, Proportion, and Substance:
Height—males, 24½ to 27½ inches at withers; females, 23½ to 26½ inches.

During World War I, the Germans invaded Flanders and Belgium. Many Bouviers helped their owners escape from the Germans by guarding and protecting them. Though some dogs had to be left behind, others were smuggled out. They went to work in the Belgian army as guard dogs, ambulance pullers, and messengers. Today's Bouviers work as herders, police dogs, and assistance dogs for the handicapped, as well as gentle family companions.

Briard

EXCERPTS FROM THE STANDARD

General Appearance:
Vigorous and alert, powerful, agile.

Size, Proportion, and Substance:
Height—males, 23 to 27 inches at withers; females, 22 to 25½ inches.

Some people say the Briard (BREE-ard) gets his name because he originated in Brie, France, the town famous for its cheese. Others say the dog was named after a thirteenth century nobleman named Aubry de Mondidier, who built a cathedral in honor of the brave and loyal dog. Wherever the name came from, this breed is centuries old and has been beloved by the French since the Middle Ages.

His most common job has always been herding. He will push people with his head to show them which way he wants them to go, and his acute hearing makes him an excellent watchdog.

The Briard has a strong character, and is happiest leading a busy, active life. This big dog thinks for himself, so training may take patience. Like most sheepdogs, Briards are wary of strangers, canine or human.

The Briard's coat is six inches long. It needs brushing and combing almost every day. He can be any solid color except white; he is usually black, gray, or tawny. He has big, dark eyes; ears are natural or cropped.

FRANCE

Collie

Collies began tending sheep in Scotland and northern England hundreds of years ago. Some believe they were called "coaly" dogs because their coats were mostly black as coal, with white. The name gradually became "Collie." Since then, writer Albert Payson Terhune's Collie stories and the Lassie movies have firmly established this breed as one of the most beloved and loyal of dogs.

SCOTLAND/ENGLAND

Collies are smart dogs with natural herding and protecting abilities. Like all working dogs, Collies need organized activities to thrive. Trained with a gentle, loving hand, they will learn quickly and happily.

Collies are active, proud, and cautious. The Collie will be content in the country or the city, as long as he has family companionship. The Collie listens to people and understands their moods; they are especially fond of children.

Collies come in rough (long) or smooth (short) coats. Both require daily brushing when shedding.

FUN FACTS

Two men once wanted to buy a Collie named Shep, who worked herding sheep on a Missouri farm. But first they wanted to test the dog's abilities.

While Shep was leading the sheep to the yard, the farmer, when Shep couldn't see him, took one of the sheep into the woods and tied it to a tree. When the gate to the farmyard was opened for the sheep to go in, Shep, as always, watched them carefully. As the last sheep entered, Shep immediately became agitated. He dashed out into the countryside and quickly located the sheep hidden in the woods. The men were impressed and offered a large amount of money for the dog.

"No," said the farmer smiling. "I'd never part with Shep. I just wanted you to see why."

EXCERPTS FROM THE STANDARD

General Appearance:
A strong, responsive, active dog; graceful and fast, with high intelligence. Impressive.

Size, Proportion, and Substance:
Height—males, 24 to 26 inches at withers; females, 22 to 24 inches. Weight—males, 60 to 75 pounds; females, 50 to 65 pounds.

German Shepherd Dog

For nobility of character, purpose, and appearance, few animals can surpass the German Shepherd Dog. This breed's courage, steadfast heart, and keen senses have endeared him to mankind—for avalanche and earthquake search and rescue, narcotics and bomb detection, tracking missing persons, and guiding the blind. He is the world's leading guard, police, and military dog, probably owing to his steady nerves.

The German Shepherd Dog also makes a wonderful companion. He is active, but dignified, and will delight in joining you in fishing, swimming, or hiking. He's very fond of children once he gets to know them. Experienced owners know just how far to assert their authority over this dog in training.

German Shepherd Dogs are descended from various old breeds of German herding and farm dogs. They can live almost anywhere as long as they get exercise and attention.

The German Shepherd Dog's outer coat is harsh; it is of medium length. He sheds profusely and needs brushing every other day, year round. The coat is usually tan with a black muzzle and "saddle" over back and sides, but any rich color is allowed.

FUN FACTS

Bob of Carmel, California, was a famous German Shepherd Dog who learned many skills. He could wipe his feet on the doormat, take money to the grocery store and pick out what he wanted to buy, balance a glass of water on his nose, and other tricks. His most unusual achievement was learning to play the piano. He held the toy piano steady with one paw, while he tapped out tunes with the other. He had his own toy piano, which he would play while "singing" along.

GERMANY

EXCERPTS FROM THE STANDARD

General Appearance:
Strong, agile, muscular, alert and full of life. Never timid or nervous. Longer than tall. Unmistakably noble and intelligent.

Size, Proportion, and Substance:
Height—males, 24 to 26 inches at withers; females, 22 to 24 inches.

Old English Sheepdog

At first he looks like a shaggy bear who tumbles around like a clown. But underneath all that hair is a sturdy worker that English farmers have valued for many years.

Old English Sheepdogs were especially skilled in guiding sheep and cattle herds from farms to the towns where they would be sold. The dogs needed to be smart, able to predict the sheep or cattle's behavior, and quick enough to round them up if they got away. Old English Sheepdogs are believed to be descended from Bearded Collies of Scotland and, possibly, a Russian dog brought to England by sailors.

In today's families, the Old English Sheepdog is a big, lovable companion. He likes to be with his family and get plenty of exercise every day.

Although the Old English Sheep-dog's abundant coat might seem a problem in hot weather, it's an effective insulator in both hot and cold. The outer coat should be hard and shaggy. The undercoat is a soft, waterproof covering that sheds out. He'll need daily brushing and combing. Color can be any shade of gray, grizzle, blue, or blue merle with or without white markings.

EXCERPTS FROM THE STANDARD

General Appearance:
A strong, compact dog, profusely coated, thickset, and muscular.

Size, Proportion, and Substance:
Height—males, 22 inches or more at the withers; females, 21 inches or more.

FUN FACTS

The Old English Sheepdog's nickname is the Bobtail. His tail is docked very close to the body about three to four days after birth. Since he worked as a "drover" dog, herding cattle and sheep to market towns, the Old English Sheepdog's tail was "bobbed" to show tax collectors that he was a working dog. Only Sporting dogs, owned by noblemen hunters, were taxed. The Old English can do more than drive herds. He has also been used as a retriever, sled dog, and watchdog.

ENGLAND

Puli

The Puli (POO-lee) is a Hungarian herding dog with a corded coat. He has a lively and impish personality.

The Puli originated more than one thousand years ago when tribes from Asia invaded Hungary, bringing their sheepdogs with them. These sheepdogs bred with various French and German herding breeds, and the result was the Puli. Since that time, shepherds have valued the dog's bravery in chasing away wolves or humans who try to grab one of their sheep. They herd animals like pigs and cattle, too. They may even try to herd toddlers with a gentle tug at their diapers.

The Puli's unusual coat has a natural tendency to "cord." At around nine months, the cords begin forming as the soft undercoat wraps around the new straight and longer outer coat. Separating the cords with fingers for about a month gets the cords going correctly. The Puli can be corded or brushed out. It is a rusty black, black, white, or shades of gray.

FUN FACTS

The Puli resembles his cousin the Komondor. Both are Hungarian sheepdogs. The Komondor quietly guarded the flock from a distance, while the smaller Puli busily kept the animals where they were supposed to be. Komondorok (plural for Komondor) were white, to stand out in the vast landscape (especially at night). The Puli's black coat helped the shepherd spot him quickly among the white sheep. The plural of Puli is Pulik.

EXCERPTS FROM THE STANDARD

General Appearance:
Medium sized, vigorous, alert, and active. With a distinctive coat and light-footed movements.

Size, Proportion, and Substance:
Height—males, 17 inches at withers; females, 16 inches.

HUNGARY

Shetland Sheepdog

The Shetland Sheepdog is better known as the "Sheltie." He is a miniature Collie developed on the Shetland Islands, located northeast of Scotland. The original Collies of Scotland were medium-size dogs, probably resembling Border Collies. From this type, the larger dogs were developed to create the Collies of today, and the smaller ones became the Shelties.

Because of his small size, the beautiful Sheltie can be happy in the city or country. He may not need as much space as a Collie, but he needs just as much attention. These intelligent, loving, and sensitive dogs become deeply attached to their families. Shelties are famous for their learning ability. Besides being smart, they want to please. Training is a pleasure; a light hand is all that is required. They like to be clean, too, and are easily housetrained. They usually get along well with gentle and thoughtful children.

This sweet, clever, and bright little dog comes wrapped in a lovely, big coat, almost identical to the bigger Collie's—except in size, of course. The outer coat is straight and harsh. It stands out from the softer, woolly undercoat. He needs brushing every other day, daily when shedding.

The small Collie dog was better suited to the harsh island life of Shetland. Food was scarce, and smaller animals survived better since they needed less food. That's why Shetland ponies are also small.

The Sheltie is called the Shetland Sheepdog instead of the Shetland Collie so that people will know it is a separate breed from the Collie.

SHETLAND ISLANDS

EXCERPTS FROM THE STANDARD

General Appearance:
Small, alert, rough-coated, agile.

Size, Proportion, and Substance:
Height—13 to 16 inches at the withers.

Welsh Corgi, Cardigan

The Cardigan Welsh Corgi entered Wales with the wild, warrior Celts three thousand years ago. Celts and Corgis both originated in central Europe. Corgis were trusted guardians of children and valued as part of the family. Their center of development was in mid-Cardiganshire, in Wales. Corgi is Welsh for "Dwarf" (*Cor*) "dog" (*gi*). He is believed to have descended from the same ancestor as the Dachshund.

The Cardigan Welsh Corgi likes to keep busy. An even temper and adaptability are his best qualities. He likes going along with his family on their activities. He tends to be somewhat serious. He is suspicious of strangers but gets along well with other animals, though he's an avid mouse catcher.

His coat needs brushing once a week. It can be all shades of red, sable, or brindle; black with or without tan or brindle points; and blue merle with or without tan or brindle points.

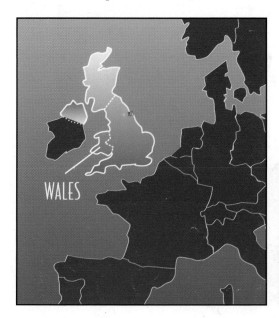

WALES

EXCERPTS FROM THE STANDARD

General Appearance:
Low set with moderately heavy bone and deep chest. Powerful, small, speedy, with a fox-like tail.

Size, Proportion, and Substance:
Height—10 1/2 to 12 1/2 inches at withers. Length—36 to 43 inches from tip of nose to tip of tail. Weight—males, 30 to 38 pounds; females, 25 to 34 pounds.

FUN FACTS

Even though the Cardigan Welsh Corgi may resemble the Pembroke Welsh Corgi, they actually had different origins. Over the years they were bred to one another and so developed similar appearances. The Cardigan Welsh Corgi is the more countrified of the two: He's a bit bigger and heavier, and his coat is slightly rougher. Also, he has a tail.

The Pembroke Welsh Corgi trots confidently into a room, having no idea that he is probably the smallest one there. He is curious, and happily approaches people and animals, even if he's never met them before. He makes friends easily.

The Pembroke Corgi is a lively companion. He plays games and enjoys traveling, visiting, even obedience training. He is glad to be in the city or the country, as long as his family is nearby.

Like Cardigan Corgis, Pembrokes were developed to herd cattle away from their master's land. Of the two types of Corgis, the Pembroke is the more recent, and came to Wales from Flanders, in the Netherlands. You can tell the two breeds apart by the Pembroke's docked tail and finer coat. His legs are straighter and his ears more pointed at the tips.

Pembroke Corgis have a thick, glossy double coat, with the softer layer underneath. It sheds year round. Brushing every other day is needed to keep the coat looking its best. Colors are red, sable, fawn, or black and tan. He may have white on his face, chest, and legs.

FUN FACTS

Pembroke Welsh Corgis have been the favorite dogs of British royalty since the late 1930s, when King George VI bought one for his daughters Elizabeth and Margaret Rose. Today, Queen Elizabeth II is often photographed with her Pembrokes.

EXCERPTS FROM THE STANDARD

General Appearance:
Low-set, strong, sturdy, and active. Bold, but kindly; intelligent and interested.

Size, Proportion, and Substance:
Height—10 to 12 inches at withers. Weight—males, 30 pounds or less; females, 28 pounds or less.

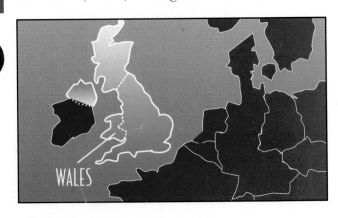

WALES

MISCELLANEOUS CLASS

The AKC currently includes 140 breeds of dogs in its registry, but there are actually hundreds of breeds that exist throughout the world. It takes time to become one of the breeds that the AKC "recognizes," or includes in its Stud Book records and competitive activities.

Owners of a breed must get together to prove their interest in getting AKC recognition for their breed. This interest must represent the entire United States.

How does a breed become recognized? The first step is to form a national or "parent" club to represent the breeders and owners. These people organize activities for their breed, such as showing or field competitions. They also determine the breed standard—an exact description of what the dog should be like. When the AKC has seen that the parent club has enthusiasm for gaining wider recognition for their breed, it might invite the parent club to join the AKC as part of the Miscellaneous Class.

Being in the Miscellaneous Class means the breed can participate in AKC obedience trials and earn titles. Miscellaneous breeds can also take part in dog shows for conformation, competing in the Miscellaneous Class, but are ineligible for championship points. Once the AKC has seen the active participation of a healthy breed over a period of time, the breed can then become "recognized" by the AKC.

Presently, the breeds in the Miscellaneous Class are:

Anatolian Shepherd Dog   **Havanese**

Australian Kelpie   **Lowchen**

Canaan Dog   **Spinone Italiano**

Anatolian Shepherd Dog

Australian Kelpie

Canaan Dog

Havanese

Lowchen

Spinone Italiano

Part 3

Your
Healthy
Dog

Chapter 6

Basic Health Concerns

This dog is the picture of health because he is well cared for in every way. *(Australian Shepherd)*

Good health brings out the best in your dog. When he's in top form, he looks good, feels good, and is ready to learn, have fun, and spend a happy life being your best friend. You can help your dog stay healthy by taking him to the veterinarian for regular checkups and vaccinations and by giving him nutritious food, exercise, training, grooming—and lots of love and hugs.

Even if you take the best possible care of your dog, he will still have days when something happens and he doesn't feel well. Since your dog can't tell you how he's feeling, it's up to you to be observant and notice when he's "off."

This section explains basic care requirements and describes some medical conditions and illnesses to which dogs are prone. Use this information to give your dog the regular care he needs and to help identify what may be wrong when your dog's not feeling well. Do not use the advice here as a substitute for consulting your veterinarian.

What a Healthy Dog Looks Like

Like every one of us, each dog is an individual. What may be normal for one dog may not be for another. You and your veterinarian will know your dog best, and you'll be able to tell when he's not feeling 100 percent. In general, the following describes the physical state of a healthy dog.

You can examine your dog's skin more closely by pushing back the hair with one hand. You will also be able to feel the coat's texture this way. *(Rottweiler)*

Skin

Healthy skin is flexible and smooth, without scabs, growths, white flakes, or red areas. It ranges in color from pale pink to brown or black depending on the breed. Spotted skin is normal, whether the dog has a spotted coat or is solid in color. Check your dog for fleas, ticks, lice, or other external parasites. To do this, blow gently on your dog's stomach or brush hair backward in a few places to see if any small specks (fleas) scurry away or if ticks are clinging to the skin. Black "dirt" on your dog's skin or bedding may be a sign of flea droppings, which means he could have fleas.

Coat

A healthy coat—short or long—is glossy and pliable, without dandruff, bald spots, or excessive oiliness.

Eyes

Healthy eyes are bright and shiny. Mucus and watery tears are normal but should be minimal and clear. The pink lining of the eyelids should not be inflamed, swollen, or have a yellow discharge. Sometimes you can see your dog's third eyelid, a light membrane, at the inside corner of an eye. It may slowly come up to cover his eye as he goes to sleep. The whites of your dog's eyes should not be yellowish. Eyelashes should not rub the eyeball. If your dog is a longhaired breed, be sure to check for this.

Your dog's eyes should be clear and bright with no swelling around them and no unusual discharge.
(Pembroke Welsh Corgi)

Ears

The skin inside your dog's ears should be light pink and clean. There should be some yellow or brownish wax, but a large amount of wax or crust is abnormal. There should be no redness or swelling inside the ear, and your dog shouldn't scratch his ears or shake his ears frequently. Dogs with long,

Healthy ears are pink inside, with no foul odor and no excessive waxy buildup. *(Pembroke Welsh Corgi)*

No doggy breath here! Just clean teeth and gums. *(Collie)*

hairy ears, like Cocker Spaniels, need extra attention to keep the ears dry and clean, inside and out.

Nose

A dog's nose is usually cool and moist. It can be black, pink, or self-colored (the same color as the coat), depending on the breed. The liquid coming out should be clear, never yellowish, thick, bubbly, or foul smelling. By the way, a cool, wet nose does not necessarily mean that the dog is healthy, and a dry, warm nose doesn't necessarily mean he's unhealthy. Taking his temperature will tell you for sure.

Mouth, Teeth, and Gums

Healthy gums are firm and pink, black, or spotted, just like the dog's skin. Young dogs have smooth white teeth that tend to darken with age. Puppies have 23 baby teeth (no molars) and adults have 42 permanent teeth, depending on the breed. As adult teeth come in, they push baby teeth out of the mouth. When puppies lose their teeth, they often swallow them. That's why you don't always find them around the house.

To check your dog's mouth, talk to him gently, then put your hand over the muzzle and lift up the sides of his mouth. Check that adult teeth are coming in as they should, and not being crowded by baby teeth that have not yet grown in. Make sure the gums are healthy and the breath is not foul smelling. Look for soft white matter or hard white, yellow, or brown matter. This is plaque or tartar and should be removed.

Mouth infections can lead to serious problems in the gums and other parts of the body, including the heart. So it's important that you give your dog's teeth and mouth special attention. (Instructions on cleaning are given in the section on grooming in this chapter.)

Temperature

One of the nicest things about dogs, especially in cold weather, is that they are warmer than we are. Their normal temperature is 101 to 102.5 degrees Fahrenheit (38.3 to 39.2 degrees Celcius).

Taking the Temperature: To take your dog's temperature you'll need a rectal thermometer. Shake the mercury down, then put some petroleum jelly on the metal-tipped end. Ask someone to hold your dog's head while you lift his tail and insert the thermometer about an inch or so into the rectum (this will depend on the size of your dog). Keep hold of the thermometer! Keep it in for three minutes. Wipe it with a tissue when you pull it out so you can read it clearly. (Adult supervision is essential.)

Heartbeat and Pulse

Because dogs come in a wide range of sizes, their heartbeats vary. A normal heart beats from 50 to 130 times a minute in a resting dog. Puppies and small dogs have faster speeds, and large dogs in top condition have slower heartbeats.

To check your dog's heartbeat, place your fingers over the left side of his chest, where you can feel the strongest beat.

To check the pulse, which is the same speed as the heartbeat, press gently on the inside of the top of the hind leg (the thigh). There is an artery there and the skin is thin, so it's easy to feel the pulse.

Elimination

Always a good indicator of a dog's health, the urine should be a clear yellow. Most adult dogs have one or two bowel movements a day. Stools should be brown and firm. What goes into the dog's mouth has a definite effect on what comes out the other end. That's why it's important to keep your dog on the food he's used to, especially during any changes in routine such as travel or moving. Runny, watery, or bloody stools, straining, or too much or too little urination or bowel movements are signals to call your veterinarian.

Weight

A healthy dog's weight is the result of the balance between diet and exercise. If he is getting enough nutritious food and exercise and is underweight or overweight, he may have a health problem. Don't let your dog get fat by giving him too many between-meal snacks; obese dogs often develop

If your dog is the proper weight, you should be able to feel his ribs—even under a lot of hair. *(Shetland Sheepdog)*

serious health problems. Before changing your dog's food, ask your veterinarian to examine him.

Is Your Dog Overweight? The best way to tell if your dog's too fat is to feel his rib-cage area. Can you feel the ribs below the surface of the skin without feeling a lot of padding? When you look at your dog from above, is the area around his ribs and down his back lean or does it bulge?

Maintaining Your Dog's Health

Grooming

Good grooming helps a dog look and feel his best. During routine grooming sessions, you'll be able to examine your dog's coat, teeth, ears, eyes, and nails. How often and how much time is necessary to do the job depends upon the breed and condition of the dog, his size, and type of coat. You can see examples of good grooming in the coats of purebred dogs at shows.

Brush your dog regularly to keep him looking his best. *(Golden Retriever)*

A Grooming Routine

Brushing several times a week keeps the average dog neat and clean, although daily attention is better. Brush all the way down to the skin, letting the massaging action stimulate blood circulation and loosen and remove flakes of dandruff.

The kind of equipment you need depends on your dog's coat texture and length. Longhaired dogs need pin brushes, which have long, round-ended stainless-steel or chrome-plated pins. Short-, medium-, and some long-coated breeds need bristle brushes. There are also slicker brushes for removing mats and dead hair; rubber curry combs to polish smooth coats and remove dead hair; clippers, stripping knives, hair dryers, and other grooming tools.

When brushing, always check for burrs and other stubborn plant materials; mats, which most frequently form behind the ears and under legs; and any cuts or scrapes on the skin itself.

Assorted grooming tools, left to right: slicker brush, combs, pin brush, shedding blade, rubber curry comb.

When bathing, work the shampoo into a lather from the neck back.

Handling and examining your dog's feet often will make nail-trimming time more pleasant. *(Rottweiler)*

All dogs shed, though some definitely more than others. Regular brushing will help keep shedding under control.

Giving your dog a bath is not something you'll need to do frequently, though you should do it regularly. Frequent washing removes natural oils and causes the coat to become dry and harsh.

When necessary, use a mild shampoo formulated for dogs. Stand the dog in a tub or basin, put cotton balls in his ears and a couple drops of mineral oil in his eyes, and you're ready. Wet the dog with warm— not hot—water, apply shampoo from the neck back, and work into a lather. Make sure you rinse your dog thoroughly with warm water, and try to get a towel around him before he gives his first shake. Rub vigorously with the towel, then blow-dry the dog if necessary and comb or brush as required.

Nail Trimming

A dog's nails should be trimmed so that they just clear the floor (if you hear them clicking, they're too long). To trim the nails, use a specially designed clipper. Some have safety guards to keep you from cutting the nails too short. You want to trim just the ends, before the "quick," which is a blood vessel inside the nail. You can see where the quick ends on a white nail, but not on a dark nail. Clip only the hook-like part of the nail that turns down.

Many dogs dislike having their nails trimmed. You can make it a painless procedure by getting your dog used to having his feet handled in puppyhood. Start trimming gently, a nail or two at a time, and your dog will learn you're not going to hurt him. If you do cut the quick, don't worry. Stop the bleeding with some styptic powder. If you find it impossible to clip your dog's nails, take him to the veterinarian or a groomer.

- Brush your dog's coat down toward the tail, then back toward the head, then down again. This loosens the dead hairs, and your dog's face will show you how good it feels.
- Many ideas have been tried, but the only way to reduce shedding is through regular brushing. Just because a dog has short hair doesn't mean he won't shed!
- For salt, mud, tree sap, burrs, or paint in your dog's coat, apply vegetable or mineral oil to the affected area for 24 hours, then wash away with soap and water. If necessary, clip away the damaged hair. *Never use gasoline, turpentine, kerosene, or any other chemical to clean tar or paint from the coat*—these chemicals are more harmful to the dog than the tar or paint.
- Mats should be gently combed out by separating the individual hairs with fingers or a comb. Then you can brush through the entire coat. If mats are too big or hard to manage, they should be carefully cut out.
- To trim your dog's nails, use a proper dog nail clipper, not regular scissors. These can crush the nail and leave ragged edges.
- Another way to keep plaque and tartar down is by making sure your dog eats a top-quality dry dog food and has tough chewing toys.

Cleaning Ears

You need to clean your dog's ears at least once a month, more often if he's prone to ear problems. To do so, cover your finger with a damp towel or use a cotton swab soaked in mineral oil. Clean only the part of the outer ear that you can see; never force anything into the ear. Some dogs need the hair plucked just inside the ear to keep air circulating and infections down. Ask your veterinarian how much and how often to do this. Also, tell your vet about any signs of infection.

Cleaning Eyes

Be careful not to get anything irritating in your dog's eyes. Clean slight discharges with a moist cotton ball. If you notice anything unusual, have your veterinarian check it out and tell you how to treat it.

Cleaning Teeth

Give your dog's teeth frequent cleanings with special toothbrushes and toothpaste designed for dogs. If your dog balks at having his teeth brushed, get him used to it by rubbing his teeth and gums with your finger. Then put a little of the doggy toothpaste on your finger and let him sniff and lick it. Then do the same with the toothbrush. Now he's ready to have you clean his teeth. Also, make sure he has toys that help clean his teeth as he chews. As your dog gets older, he may have a buildup of tartar that requires special cleaning by your veterinarian.

Anal Sacs

Anal sacs are located on each side of your dog's anus. If you notice your dog scooting along on his rear end or licking or scratching his anus, he may have impacted anal sacs. These are the glands surrounding the anus that exude scent when your dog has a bowel movement. Ask your veterinarian how to treat an anal sac problem.

Nutrition and Feeding

A good diet will keep your dog looking and feeling his best. It provides your dog with the right amounts of essential nutrients: proteins, carbohydrates, fats, vitamins, minerals, and water. Your dog must have all these in correct proportions to stay healthy. Dog food companies know this, and make a variety of foods for all a dog's life stages, from puppyhood to senior citizenship.

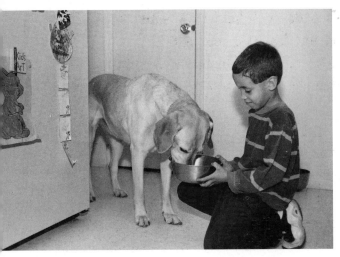

A good diet is essential to your dog's health. *(Labrador Retriever)*

With so many dog foods on the market, it's tough to know what's right for your dog. You can ask a breeder or your veterinarian for advice, then it's up to you to see how the food affects your dog. If your dog's energy level is right for his breed, if his skin and coat are healthy, if his stools are firm and brown and he fits the bill of a healthy dog as described in this chapter, then the food is doing its job. Remember, when it comes to feeding your dog, you often get what you pay for, so don't skimp.

Types of Food

Many owners prefer to feed kibbled (dry), rather than soft dog food for several reasons. Crunching the hard kibbles helps keep your dog's teeth clean and exercises his chewing muscles. Also, it benefits the owner by keeping the dog's stools compact and firm for easy cleanup. If your dog prefers the tastier, soft food, you can mix some in with the kibble. The most common proportions are three-quarters kibble with one-quarter canned food. Semi-moist foods, while convenient, don't offer the nutritional benefits of premium kibble or canned foods.

When, How Much, and How Often to Feed

Puppies need more calories and essential nutrients than do adult dogs. Choose a food specially formulated for puppies. Puppies under six months should get three or four meals a day. They are growing rapidly, but their stomachs can't hold much. After six months they can go to two or three meals a day. Your dog's breeder can advise you on what's appropriate for your breed.

Adult dogs should be fed according to their size and energy needs. Again, your breeder can give you the best advice for your breed of dog.

Most adults should get two meals a day of whatever quantity suits them. Feeding two meals a day seems to keep dogs more content.

All dogs need separate food and water bowls. The bowls should be cleaned daily, and cool, fresh water should be available *at all times.*

Treats and Supplements

Dog bowls come in a variety of shapes and sizes. Your dog will need separate bowls for food and water.

Dogs can be great beggars, but don't let yours charm you into the habit of sharing your food. Dogs' nutritional needs are different from humans', and you aren't doing your best friend any favor by giving him a diet meant for you. There are plenty of nutritious dog treats on the market. Be sure to feed them as part of the dog's overall food intake. Dogs also love vegetables such as broccoli, carrots, zucchini, cauliflower, peas, and beans, and fruits such as bananas, grapes, apples, and melon. These make great treats.

Because commercial foods are nutritionally complete, most veterinarians advise against supplementing a healthy dog's diet. However, all dogs are individuals and yours may need something special. Consult with your veterinarian and read more about canine nutrition in books and magazine articles that specialize in the subject.

What *Not* to Feed

Never give your dog chocolate. It contains a chemical, theobromine, that is toxic to dogs. Also, don't feed your dog bones that can splinter or that have sharp edges. Large, hard bones such as knuckle and marrow bones are fine, but parboil them before feeding to destroy harmful parasites, and take them from your dog if he starts to actually eat the bone rather than just chew on it.

Chapter 7

Preventive Care

With regular medical care, you and your dog will spend many happy years together. *(English Toy Spaniel, left, and Pointer)*

The old adage "An ounce of prevention is worth a pound of cure" is true of your dog's health as well. That's why you want to groom him regularly, feed him the best food, and make sure he gets enough exercise.

You also need to take your dog to the veterinarian for regular checkups, during which he will be checked for internal parasites and given his regular shots. External parasites such as fleas and ticks can be eliminated before they become a serious problem. You may also want to consider spaying or neutering. All these things will be discussed in this chapter.

Vaccinations: What and When

Regular vaccinations (shots) from your veterinarian can keep your dog from getting serious and sometimes fatal illnesses such as distemper, parvovirus, hepatitis, leptospirosis, coronavirus, and rabies. A vaccination is also available for kennel cough, a respiratory problem that affects young dogs or dogs exposed to many other dogs.

A puppy's first vaccines ideally should be given at five or six weeks of age and continue over a period of several weeks, up to sixteen weeks. Afterward, yearly booster shots provide the protection your dog will need. Be sure to stick to the schedule your veterinarian gives you to insure immunity.

Internal Parasites

These are worms, specifically, hookworms, roundworms, tapeworms, whipworms, and heartworms. Your veterinarian will prescribe medication to clear up any infestations, but the sooner they're caught, the better.

Hookworms are common in puppies, though dogs of any age can be infested. Hookworms are acquired by puppies from their mother by nursing and by adult dogs by swallowing the parasite's eggs or having the hookworm burrow into the skin. The veterinarian will ask you to bring a stool sample to your checkups so he or she can look for hookworms under the microscope. Infection can be prevented by keeping your dog's environment clean.

Roundworms are also common in puppies and can infect other dogs and children. They look like white, firm, rounded strips of thin spaghetti, one to three inches long. Your veterinarian will look for signs of roundworms in the stool sample. Keep your dog's environment sanitized to prevent these worms from spreading.

Tapeworms will cause your dog to lose weight and have occasional diarrhea. You'll know if your dog's got them because you'll see segments of the worms around his anus or on his stool. The segments look like grains of rice.

Whipworms are acquired by licking or sniffing contaminated ground. They live in the dog's intestine and are only detectable in a stool sample.

Heartworms enter a dog's bloodstream from the bite of an infected mosquito. The worms mature in the dog's heart, growing to twelve inches in length and effectively clogging the heart—a very serious condition. Heartworm infection occurs throughout the United States but is particularly common in warm, mosquito-infested areas. Treatment is expensive and can be dangerous. Fortunately, prevention is simple these days. The dog is first tested for heartworms to be sure there are none in his system, then he's put on a schedule of heartworm preventive pills. These are given once a day or once a month, depending on the type of medication.

Your veterinarian will put your puppy on a vaccination schedule so he won't get infectious diseases when he's out in the big world. *(Golden Retriever)*

Puppies often inherit worms from their mothers, but the veterinarian will check and give you medicine to clear them up quickly. *(French Bulldog)*

External Parasites

Fleas

Fleas are a very common problem, but that doesn't mean they're acceptable! You will need to be diligent about flea control, but if you're not, your dog can suffer hair loss, allergic reactions, and worms. You risk infesting your house, too, which means you and your family can become flea meals as well.

Look for fleas when you groom your dog (as discussed in chapter 6). If you see any, you will need to treat your dog and your dog's environment. There are numerous products available for this. Ask your veterinarian which would work best for you and your dog.

Ticks

These parasites cause a number of serious illnesses, including Rocky Mountain spotted fever and Lyme disease. Check your dog for ticks daily if he spends any time outside, and whenever you see one take it off immediately. The best way to do this is to numb the tick with rubbing alcohol or petroleum jelly, then pull it off with tweezers. If it bursts in your fingers you could become infected. Once removed, kill the tick by putting it in a container of alcohol. Prevent an infestation by treating your dog with a tick powder, dip, or spray recommended by your veterinarian.

Dogs love the great outdoors, but it's your job to check them for fleas, ticks, and other parasites when it's time to come back inside. (Border Collies)

Lice, Mites, and Mange

These are all microscopic organisms that feed on your dog's skin and cause itching, hair loss, and infection.

Lice live in a dog's hair and can be killed by dipping with an insecticide effective against ticks or fleas.

Various kinds of mites inhabit different areas of the dog, and the problems they cause are generally known as mange. Ear mites live in the dog's ears. Your dog may have mites if he shakes his head and scratches his ears. Scabies, which affects humans as well as dogs, is caused when mites burrow into the dog's skin and cause intense itching and hair loss. Scabies usually affects the ears, elbows, legs, and face. Demodectic mange causes

The most effective way to give your dog a pill is to open his mouth and place it all the way in the back, as this girl is doing. *(Border Terrier)*

hair loss around the forehead, eyes, muzzle, and forepaws. It's caused by a mite that lives in hair follicles and causes hair loss, thick, red skin, and infected areas. There is also a mite that causes "walking dandruff" on a dog's head, back, and neck. This mite also causes itchy red spots on humans. All mites should be diagnosed from a skin scraping by a veterinarian.

Giving Your Dog Medicine

You shouldn't have a problem giving your dog the pills, liquid, or ointment prescribed by your veterinarian. Just follow instructions and be firm but kind.

The easiest way to give a pill or liquid is to disguise it in the dog's food, but this doesn't always work because the dog will recognize it and not eat it. Try concealing it in a treat such as a piece of cheese and popping it into your dog's mouth.

The most effective and simplist method is to put the medicine directly into the dog's mouth. To give a pill, open the mouth the way you would to check the teeth and gums. Place the pill all the way back in the mouth, then close the dog's mouth, hold his muzzle up, and stroke his throat until you feel him swallow. Follow up with a treat to be sure he's eaten the pill. To give liquid, use a dropper filled with the medicine, hold your dog's head steady, place the dropper into the corner of the mouth between the back teeth and squirt. Hold the dog's mouth closed so he's forced to swallow. Follow up with a treat.

Follow your veterinarian's instructions for eye or ear medications.

Spaying or Neutering Your Dog

Unless you know you are going to show your dog, it is best to have your female spayed or your male neutered. Spaying or neutering is a fail-safe method of birth control.

A spay operation removes the female dog's ovaries and uterus. A spayed female will not come into season the two or three times a year that female dogs typically do. She will not attract male dogs from miles around; she will not discharge on rugs, sofas, or her own bedding; and she will not be

A spayed or neutered dog is a great pal. *(Spinone Italiano)*

prone to diseases such as pyometra (uterine infection) and mammary cancer.

A neutered male cannot breed successfully. His desire to roam in search of females will be reduced, and he may be less aggressive in defending his territory. Also important is that he will be less susceptible to prostate cancer.

Chapter 8

Illness and First Aid

As your dog's best friend and caretaker, you'll know when he's not feeling well. *(German Wirehaired Pointer)*

Y ou and your dog are best friends, and friends watch out for each other. When your dog doesn't behave as he usually does, he is telling you something is wrong. "Listen" to what your dog says by the way he acts.

When to Call the Vet

Sometimes it's not clear that something is serious. The dog is just "off" or "not himself." That's a signal to watch closely. If you detect any of the behaviors described in the list below, it's definitely time to call your veterinarian.

If you've taken your dog for regular checkups and the vet knows you and your dog, sometimes problems can be solved over the telephone. Fast action can save your dog's life. If there's a major problem such as a car accident, snakebite, or poisoning, don't hesitate a moment. Your vet can instruct you by phone so you can start emergency treatment immediately as you rush your dog to the vet's office.

Some dogs may have congenital disorders, or defects with which they are born. Some of these problems don't show up until the dog is older. The AKC has launched the Canine Genome Project, a major effort to determine what causes these defects, with the goal of someday controlling them in purebred dogs.

If your dog exhibits any unusual behavior, including the following, call your veterinarian immediately:

- Vomiting, diarrhea, or excessive urination for more than twelve hours

- Fainting

- Loss of balance, staggering, falling

- Constipation or straining to urinate

- Runny eyes or nose

- Persistent scratching at eyes or ears

- Thick discharge from eyes, ears, nose, or sores

- Coughing or sneezing

- Difficulty breathing, prolonged panting

- Shivering

- Whining for no apparent reason

- Loss of appetite for 24 hours or more

- Weight loss

- Dramatic increase in appetite for 24 hours or more

- Increased restlessness

- Excessive sleeping or unusual lack of activity

- Limping, holding, or protecting part of the body

- Excessive drinking of water

Problems of Particular Body Systems

As explained before, this book is no substitute for the trained eye or experience of a veterinarian. However, you will notice problems that come up

A dog's skin protects its inner organs and tissues from dehydration, temperature changes, and foreign substances such as burrs. It needs to be in good condition to do its job. *(Brittany)*

with your dog, and the more specific you can be when you describe them to your vet, the better chance you'll have of getting effective treatment. Although not emergencies, these problems particular to certain parts of the body are red flags. If they worsen, call your veterinarian.

Skin Problems

The skin protects the organs and tissues within the body from invasion by foreign substances, changing temperatures, and dehydration. The skin is also responsible for processing information about the external world through sensations. The following signs may indicate allergies, parasites, underlying disease, infections, abscesses, or tumors that cause the skin to malfunction:

Itching

Red, sore, moist patches

Dandruff or dry flakes

Scabs

Hair loss

Discoloration

Swelling

Heavy or foul-smelling discharge

Lumps or bumps

Respiratory Problems

The respiratory system includes the organs involved in the breathing process: nose, mouth, and lungs. The following signs may indicate kennel cough, bronchitis, pneumonia, a foreign object caught in the windpipe or nose, a birth defect, allergies, or tumors.

Nasal discharge

Sneezing

Coughing

Noisy or difficult breathing

Voice change or loss

Abnormal chest sounds

With breeds like this Puli, whose heads are covered with hair, you have to be especially attentive to problems of the eyes, ears, and nose.

Head Problems

The head holds the dog's sensory organs of sight, hearing, and taste, as well as nasal passages lined with scent-detecting cells. The following can affect the eyes, ears, nose, mouth, and throat and can range from scratches to wounds to infections.

Eyes: Abnormal discharge; excessive or insufficient tear production; inflamed tissues; loss of vision (walking into stationary objects); growths in or around the eye; eyelids turning in or out; whiteness or opaqueness; swelling; sensitivity to light (squinting); fluttering of the iris.

Ears: Discharge or wax accumulation; foul odor; scratching; swelling or tenderness; inflammation; scabs or crusts; hearing loss; head tilt; head shaking; loss of balance.

Nose: Cut and bleeding; thick, white or colored discharge; frequent sneezing.

Mouth and throat: Discharge or excessive drooling; swollen lips, mouth, tongue, gums, throat; pawing at the mouth; head shaking; scabs; loss of appetite; bad breath; growths; bleeding; trouble swallowing; coughing or gagging.

Musculoskeletal Problems

The musculoskeletal system supports, protects, and moves the dog's body. It includes muscles, tendons, ligaments, and bones. In the bones, fats and minerals are stored and red blood cells are made. The following signs may be indications of lameness, sprains, fractures, dislocations, ligament injuries, hip dysplasia, disk disease, Lyme disease, or arthritis:

Limping	Stiffness
Weakness	Abnormal walking or running
Pain	Swelling at the joints

Heart Problems

The heart is a vital organ that pumps blood to the entire body. The following symptoms can be signals of heart disease, heartworm, or congenital defects:

Coughing and shortness of breath

Lethargy and weakness

Fainting

Weight loss

Insufficient growth

Bluish or pale gums

Swollen abdomen and legs

Irregular or rapid heartbeat

Vibrations over the heart

A dog's musculoskeletal system supports its whole body. It gives this American Staffordshire Terrier its impressive form and substance.

Gastrointestinal Problems

This system receives and processes food, from the mouth to the anus, including stomach, liver, and intestines. The following problems can be caused by factors as varied as a new food, stress, parasites, viruses, and bacteria. In dogs with long hair, the anus is sometimes blocked by matted hair. Enlarged glands or a hernia also cause blockage. A dog will also show some of these symptoms if he has swallowed an indigestible or poisonous object or substance. If you suspect poisoning, call your veterinarian *immediately* and do as he or she tells you.

Vomiting

Diarrhea

Blood or mucus in stools

Constipation

Straining

Swollen abdomen

Restlessness

Excessive gas

Scooting on bottom

Unusual drooling

Appetite and weight loss

Bad coat

Jaundice (yellowing of skin and whites of eyes)

White, black, or tar-like stools

Nervous System Problems

The following are signs of serious diseases such as tetanus, rabies, or distemper, all of which are preventable by vaccination. Other possible conditions include Lyme disease, epilepsy, spinal injury, or tumors.

Seizures

Sudden strange actions

Sudden changes in personality

Lack of coordination, falling

Weakness

Changes in muscles, stiffness

Dragging rear legs

Paralysis

Urinary System Problems

These are the signs for chronic kidney failure, bladder stones, and other diseases or infections:

Excessive drinking and urination

Straining to urinate

Frequent urination in small amounts

Inability to urinate

Inability to control urination (floor wetting)

Blood or pus in urine

Vomiting

Hunched-up position

Weight and appetite loss

Multisystem Problems

Certain extremely serious diseases or conditions involve more than one of the dog's systems. These include cancer, parvovirus, Lyme disease, diabetes, distemper, infections, protozoan illnesses, and other diseases, many of which are preventable by vaccination. That's why it's so important to keep to the schedule your veterinarian gives you for your dog's shots.

Emergencies and First Aid

It takes a skilled and practiced veterinarian to make the proper diagnosis from your dog's symptoms. But you are extremely important because you can describe in detail all the symptoms as well as the dog's recent activities. Every dog falls victim to an illness or accident at some point in his life. Your preventive care, good grooming, and careful observations will go a long way toward keeping problems manageable. Common sense also goes a long way in preventing and managing emergencies.

The three steps for first aid are: (1) Be prepared by becoming familiar with the suggestions in this chapter. (2) Alert an adult immediately in an emergency situation. (3) Call your veterinarian. The telephone number for poison control and your veterinarian (clinic and emergency) should be as handy as your own doctor's number. Know how to find the emergency clinic in case your own vet is unavailable.

What You May Need to Do in an Emergency

Restrain/Muzzle the Dog

When in pain and frightened, even the best-trained dog may panic and struggle against you. You could get bitten, so it's best to have an adult help you muzzle the dog.

Panty hose, a cotton bandage, a necktie, or piece of rope about two feet long can do the job. Tie a loose knot in the middle, leaving a large loop. Slip the loop over the dog's nose and tighten gently but firmly about halfway up the nose. Bring the ends down and knot under the dog's chin, then bring the ends behind the back of the ears and tie again.

Transport the Dog

Picking up an injured dog may cause further injury, so taking him to the vet should be done carefully. Place the animal on a piece of plywood or other hard surface to move him. Small dogs should be placed in a box. Towels or blankets can also be used as stretchers.

Artificial Respiration

This is needed when the dog is unable to breathe. This is a job for an adult because it involves mouth contact and the risk of being bitten. Also, a child's mouth may not be large enough to cover the dog's entire muzzle.

First the dog's mouth should be checked for any objects, including mucus or blood, and cleared. Then hold the mouth closed, inhale, completely cover the dog's nose with your mouth, and gently breathe out. Don't blow hard! Repeat every five to six seconds.

Heart Massage (CPR)

When the dog's heart has stopped beating, heart massage, combined with artificial respiration, can be used. This is known as CPR, or cardiopulmonary resuscitation. With the dog lying on his side, place hands over the heart area and press firmly about 70 times per minute. For small dogs, place one hand on each side of the chest near the elbow. Press gently, or ribs can break.

General Emergencies

Bleeding

If your dog is bleeding externally, apply gentle pressure with cloth, bandages, or whatever is close by—even your own hand if necessary. Don't worry about cleaning out the wound until the bleeding has stopped; otherwise, you will just allow more bleeding. Take the dog to the veterinarian as quickly as possible. Antibiotics may be needed to stave off an infection.

If the bleeding is internal, which you can't see, it can be even more dangerous. Internal bleeding usually comes from a "blunt trauma," such as injury from a car or heavy object or from a fall. The dog *may* show these signs: a painful or swollen abdomen; pale gums; or blood in vomit, urine, stools, saliva, or nose discharge. Internal hemorrhage is extremely serious and should be tended to by a veterinarian without delay.

Shock

Shock occurs when the heart and blood vessels shut down. It can result from a disease or injury. The signs are depression, rapid, weak heartbeat, dilated pupils, low temperature, and muscle weakness. Respond at once by applying a pressure bandage if the dog is bleeding, keeping the animal warm and quiet, and taking him to the veterinarian immediately.

Fractures

Dogs will hold a fractured or dislocated limb in an unnatural position; sometimes a broken bone is visible through the skin. In some cases there are multiple fractures. The dog should be transported with as little movement as possible. The sooner a fracture is treated, the better the recovery will be.

For safety's sake, put your dog in a crate while you travel with him, and don't leave him in the car alone, even if the windows are open.

Common Emergencies

Heatstroke

Heatstroke may occur when dogs are left in cars on hot, or even warm, days; when kennel areas do not have proper ventilation; or when dogs are over exercised on hot days. The signs are rapid breathing, rapid heartbeat, high body temperature (above 104 degrees Fahrenheit), and collapse.

Dogs suffering from heatstroke must be cooled down as quickly as possible. Spray him with cool water, place ice around the belly, head, and neck. Stop cooling when the dog's temperature reaches 103 degrees Fahrenheit. Call your veterinarian after administering the first aid, or better yet, have someone else call while you're treating your dog.

Vomiting and Diarrhea

These are usually the signs of problems with the digestive system, and could be caused by any number of things, from the ordinary (spicy food) to the dangerous (poison). Dehydration from vomiting or diarrhea can be fatal. Make sure the dog has plenty of water. If neither condition seems severe, feed the dog a bland diet of plain cooked chicken and rice for 12 hours. If vomiting or diarrhea persist 12 hours or more, call the vet.

Dogfights

Dogfights usually concern territory, social position, or a female in season. Despite all the fuss, they are usually finished quickly. Do not interfere. A dog will act in the heat of the moment, and may bite you in defense. Alert an adult immediately. Do not try to separate fighting dogs by hand. Use a hose or bucket of water, if available.

If the dog is bleeding, attempt to stop blood flow with pressure. Once bleeding has stopped, any wound, no matter how small, should be washed out. The dog may have internal injuries or wounds you can't see, and should be attended to by a vet.

Seizures

When a seizure occurs, the dog loses control of his muscles. He may fall on his side and seem to "paddle" the air. Surround the dog with a blanket so he won't hurt himself, but don't try to handle him, especially around the head. He may bite in a reflexive action. Call your veterinarian.

Poisoning

Have the phone number of the nearest Poison Control Center handy, along with your doctor's and vet's numbers. Time is critical with poisons. The longer the poison is in the system, the more extensive the damage. Assist the vet by bringing the label or container of the substance the dog has eaten. These are some common poisons and their effects:

Insecticides and parasite medication. Flea and tick sprays, shampoos, and collars, and worm medications must be used according to directions. Signs of overuse of these chemicals are trembling and weakness, drooling, vomiting, and loss of bowel control. Call the vet.

Rodent poisons. Most rat poisons thin the blood so it is unable to clot. Making the dog vomit before 30 minutes have gone by will usually get rid of most of the poison. Your vet can tell you how to get your dog to vomit. Poisons containing strychnine, such as those for gophers, can cause death rapidly. No poison should ever be where a dog—or a child—can get near them.

Acids, alkalis, and petroleum products. Vomiting should not be induced if these products have been swallowed. Call the vet immediately; if the vet is unavailable, you can give antacids (such as Milk of Magnesia or Pepto-Bismol)—approximately two teaspoons per five pounds of body weight—to temporarily counteract acids. For alkali ingestion, use one part vinegar to four parts water, giving as much as above.

Antifreeze. This sweet-tasting substance can leak out of parked cars, leaving an inviting puddle for wandering dogs. It is extremely toxic to dogs, even in small amounts. Call the vet immediately. And ask your parents to use one of the new animal-safe antifreezes in their own car.

Paint. Do not use turpentine or gasoline to remove paint from your dog; they are more dangerous to your dog than paint. Clip the hair if necessary.

Tar and grease. Remove with vegetable oil, then wash with gentle soap and water.

Burns. Clip away hair, gently wash with mild soap, apply antibiotic steroid ointment. Take dog to the vet.

Common Household Poisons

- Acetaminophen (Tylenol, Datril, etc.)
- Antifreeze and other car fluids
- Bleach
- Boric Acid
- Cleaning fluid
- Deodorants
- Deodorizers
- Detergents
- Disinfectants
- Drain cleaner
- Furniture polish
- Gasoline
- Hair colorings
- Weed killers
- Insecticides
- Kerosene
- Matches
- Mothballs
- Nail polish and remover
- Paint
- Perscription medicine
- Rat poison
- Rubbing alcohol
- Shoe polish
- Sleeping pills
- Snail or slug bait
- Turpentine
- Windshield-wiper fluid

A Canine First-Aid Kit

Ask your parents to help you assemble two first-aid kits for your dog. Keep one in a handy place in your house or apartment and one in the car.

- Tweezers
- Scissors
- Nail clippers
- Soft, strong tape for emergency muzzle

- Bandage

- Roll of two-inch wide adhesive bandage

- Two-inch and four-inch square gauze bandage

- Liquid antiseptic

- Tube of antiseptic cream

- Cotton balls

- Antacid

- Flea spray

- Dog shampoo

- Pediatric electrolyte solution (to be used on vet's instruction)

- Meat tenderizer (for insect and jellyfish stings)

- Antihistamine tablets (to be used on vet's instruction)

- Hydrogen peroxide (to induce vomiting; use only on vet's instruction)

- Charcoal tablets (to absorb harmful substance dog has eaten; use only on vet's instruction)

- Small jar for urine or stool sample

- Ear drops and eye drops

- Medication prescribed by your vet

Chapter 9

Training

Training is good for you *and* your dog, so don't be afraid to start young. *(Petit Basset Griffon Vendéen)*

Training your dog is an absolute necessity. Just like children, dogs come into the world filled with love and curiosity, but not manners. They need to be taught how to get along in the family. That includes eliminating outside of the house, behaving properly in the house, and being polite to people and other animals. This is a demanding, yet enjoyable job that begins the moment the dog enters your house and your life.

Training makes dogs happy. By nature, dogs prefer a society with rules, where everybody knows his place. When you teach dogs the rules of your family, they feel secure knowing exactly what they are and aren't allowed to do. Dogs will test you from time to time, to see if anything has changed. That's one reason it's so important to keep the same rules and the same schedules every day.

You Are the Trainer

You set the stage for the successful training of your dog. Your most important tool is "positive reinforcement"—getting the dog to do what you want with praise and reward. The two other critical tools are patience and firmness (never harshness). You must be confident while training, and you must be consistent. Your goal is to get the dog to respond to your request, delivered *once*, in a cheerful, business-like voice. It's up to you to set a positive, happy tone for training.

What to Expect from Your Dog

The amount of patience and firmness you will need often depends on the breed of dog. Investigate the breed you want before you get him. Breeders, veterinarians, trainers, and owners can tell you what it's like to train different breeds. Some breeds learn quickly; others require more time. Some breeds need a strong hand; others require only gentle correcting.

With all breeds, being too hard on a dog will only teach him to fear you and others. He can become overly fearful or overly aggressive. On the other hand, if you're not confident in your authority, the dog may try to take over. Tell your dog what to do, but respect him for who he is. Enroll in an obedience class for advice and support in the training process.

Praise your dog when he's done something right. Playtime with a favorite toy is a great form of praise. (Shetland Sheepdog)

Praise and Correction

Praise when right. Correct when wrong. It's as simple as that. A correction is the word "no," delivered in a firm voice. Always follow a correction with praise as soon as the mistake has been cleared up.

Make a habit of pointing out your dog's good behavior to him—he wants to please you, so he'll remember to do it again. When he does something wrong, correct him, show him the right thing to do, then praise him. For example: Puppies must chew, but when they chew on your shoe or hand, correct them; then give them a chew toy and praise.

Don't hold a grudge when the dog misbehaves. He will forget his mistake in a few minutes. If you stay angry he'll just wonder why you aren't friends anymore.

Housebreaking

The keys to success in housebreaking are determination and timing. Be patient and positive. Again, reward works far better than punishment.

TRAINING TIP: *If the puppy or dog never has the opportunity to eliminate in the house, he will never consider it a place to eliminate.*

Take a puppy outside as often as possible. Puppies need to eliminate frequently, especially 15 or 20 minutes after eating and after rigorous play. As they get older, they will be able to wait longer. Also, watch for signs such as whining or turning in a circle, then quickly pick him up and take him outside. When he eliminates outside, praise him immediately, using a word of your choice for the action (always use that word for it). Then play with him for a little while before bringing him back inside. He will learn that eliminating outside earns him praise and some extra playtime as well.

TRAINING TIP: *Even if you're in a hurry, try not to bring the dog inside immediately after he eliminates. He will figure out that as soon as he eliminates, he is taken back inside. Some dogs will try to hold it to stay outside longer. This can be frustrating on a rainy night!*

What about mistakes? They will happen in the beginning. Do not punish a dog for this or he will simply hide from you for his next in-house elimination. Instead, correct with a gentle, firm "No," take outside, say your word, and praise when he relieves himself. Then be sure you're ready the next time he needs to go.

TRAINING TIP: *Clean up where he messed in the house with white vinegar to get rid of the smell. That way, he won't return to that spot.*

A crate is an excellent aid in house-training, and also gives the dog a den of her own. *(French Bulldog)*

Using a Crate

Crates are useful for housebreaking. A dog should have a cozy place to curl up, but he should not be kept locked in a crate his entire life. For housebreaking, however, two weeks of restriction can mean a lifetime of trusted freedom in the house. Feed the dog and within a reasonable time take him outside to eliminate. Then put him in the crate with his toys and a blanket until it's time for him to eliminate again, never more than two hours for a puppy, four hours for an adult dog.

Dogs do not like to eliminate in their play and sleep areas. The crate should be large enough for him to stand up and make a full turn, but not so large that he can have an area set aside for eliminating. Once the dog is housebroken, you can leave the crate with its door open. It's a quiet place for him to relax. Kids love to play with their dogs, but sometimes the dog needs a crate break.

If you live in an apartment without easy access to the outdoors, you may need to "paper train" your puppy. To do this, choose an enclosed area in the kitchen or bathroom and cover the entire floor with paper. When he eliminates on it, replace the dirty paper with clean paper right away. In a few days, take away some of the papers to leave part of the floor bare. If he eliminates on the bare floor, correct him gently and put him on the paper, then praise. As he gets the idea, gradually remove more and more paper, until you have just a small area for elimination.

TRAINING TIP: *A good place to leave that final papered area is near the door. That is where he will eventually go to let you know that he needs to go outside. You can even replace the small paper area with a low box containing a piece of grassy sod, to start the idea of going on grass. When he's old enough to hold it longer, you can follow the regular outside method.*

The correct way to put on a training collar is to form the collar into a *P*, then put it on the dog. This girl is holding the P sideways before slipping it over her dog's head. *(Shetland Sheepdog)*

Obedience Training

When your dog is about six months old, he is probably ready for obedience training. If you have an older dog, it's never too late to start. Dogs are smart; they can learn.

Most obedience-training programs will allow children to train their own dog, but they usually ask that the same person work with the dog for all the classes. Be ready to make the time commitment, usually an hour once or twice a week. To find a class, ask your usual sources—breeders, dog clubs, vets, other owners, pet-supply stores, or local animal shelters.

In the meantime, it's a good idea to get your dog used to a training collar and leash. *Proper placement of the training collar is important.* The dog will be on your left side during training exercises, so the long part of the chain collar should run over the top of the dog's neck and to his right side, where you will attach the leash. That way the collar will slide and tighten when you pull on the leash. If you have it the wrong way around, it will tighten *but not release* when you relax the leash. That sends an uncomfortable message to the dog!

The correct way to put on and use a training collar is to form it into a P. Then, with the dog on your left, slip the collar over his head. The loop that attaches to your leash should loosen and tighten easily. The chain should be long enough to have some slack, but only a few inches longer than the size of the dog's neck.

Some dogs resist a leash at first. If yours does, to get him used to it, simply attach a short leash to the collar, and let the dog run around with it in an enclosed area. Make sure the leash doesn't get caught on anything and frighten him. Once he's used to the feeling of it, you can gently pick up the leash and handle it. Keep it fun, so the dog learns that wearing the leash leads to happy times with you, his owner.

Obedience Basics

Sit

To teach sit, put your dog or puppy on your left side. Walk along with your dog, stop, and give the command "Sit!" (1) You don't have to yell, just speak it in normal tone of voice. With your left hand, guide his rear down into a sitting position (2). Your right holds his head up and in position with the lead. When his rear end hits the floor and he's looking up at you, say "Good sit!" (3) Practice once or twice several times a day.

(1)   (2)   (3)

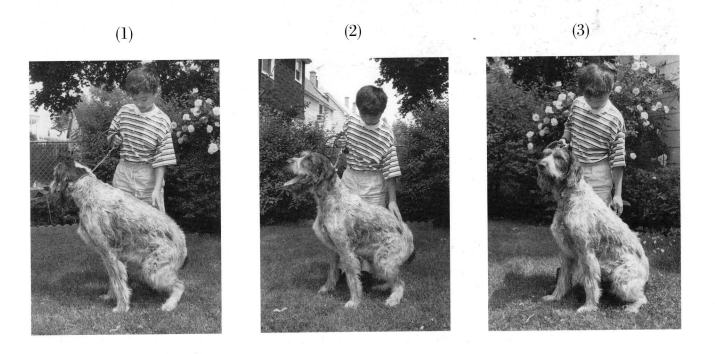

Stay

With your pup or dog on lead on your left side, tell him "Sit." When he's seated, say "Stay," and place the palm of your left hand in front of his muzzle (1). Take one step away from him, and don't try to make him stay for more than a few seconds to start off with. If he moves, guide him back into position and start over. When he will stay for just a few seconds, praise with "Good stay!" and call him to you happily. Try again, but not too often. Slowly increase the time and distance you step away from him (2) while cutting down on the continued commands until he'll stay on one command for at least three minutes. (3) With practice you'll be able to go some distance before coming back.

(1)

(2)

(3)

Down

This one also starts off with your dog or puppy sitting on your left side. Stand over or kneel beside him and take his front paws in your hands (1).

Say "Down" and gently move his paws out and down until he is in the down position (2). Tell him "Good down!" If you do this with your left arm over his back and around his body, he shouldn't want to struggle against you (3). Keep him in position for a few seconds then release him and get him into sit for another try. Practice occasionally until he goes down on command without your having to lift him. He should stay quietly until released, without any pressure of your left hand on his back. After a few days, you should be able to stand erect and give only one command, "Down," to have him lie at your side.

(1)

(2)

(3)

Come

This is probably the most important command your dog can learn. With your puppy or dog walking at your side, take a sudden step back and say your dog's name followed by "Come!" As you call him, snap the lead to turn him around and get him headed back to you. Make it fun. When he's facing you, keep walking backward, urging him along. The key to success with "Come" is that there is never a contest of brute strength between you and your dog. He should already be in motion when you first give him the "Come" while walking, and you should be happily encouraging him to join you. Never call your dog to come when you're angry or he will associate coming to you with something negative.

(1)

(2)

(3)

A polished "Come." The dog is on a sit-stay at the end of a long lead, is called to come, and runs toward the encouraging voice of his owner.

Heel

To begin heeling, put the dog on your left side and start to walk by calling his name and giving the command to heel: "Fido, heel!" Give the command just as you take the first step, and simultaneously give a light snap on the leash to persuade him to come along. Remember to step off with your left leg first; this tells your dog you're ready to go (1).

As you walk along, continue to urge him to walk at your left side, with his neck and shoulder aligned with your left leg. Praise when he gets it right: "Good heel!" (2) It takes a while for the dog to learn this one. Practice in brief but lengthening sessions two or more times daily until you have to give only one command as you start walking (3).

An obedience instructor will give you more advice; it's best to learn with an experienced teacher, and a class setting helps your dog learn how to get along with others. Here are some tips to help you along the way.

(1)   (2)   (3)

Start the heel with your dog sitting on your left. Lead with your left foot, saying "Heel," and begin walking. Give a tug on the leash if your dog pulls ahead and encourage him to stay at your side.

Training Tips

- Practice the training lesson for about 10 minutes once or twice a day.

- Keep training positive and fun. Stop if you feel bored or frustrated, and try again later.

- Play with your dog after training.

- Use the dog's name with movement exercises.

- If using a training collar, tighten with short, quick pulls only, not a long steady pull—that can hurt the dog.

With advanced training, your dog will learn to respond to hand signals as well as voice commands. This is the command for down, and you can see the dog complying. *(Brittany)*

- Give commands once, with kindness and firmness. No pleading or yelling.

- Praise after every completed command. This is what the dog is working for. You cannot praise too much.

- For the sit, run your hand along the dog's back and behind his tail, and gently push behind the knee, where the back leg naturally bends, saying "Sit." Don't push down on your dog's hips.

- Your trainer will teach you the come command. *It is one of the most important for your dog's safety.* However, in the meantime, if your dog won't come when you call, don't chase him or get mad at him. That will give him the wrong message. Keep him on a leash until he will come properly, and always praise when he comes.

- Stay hopeful. Training takes time. Believe in your ability to get the job done, and believe in your dog's intelligence and ability to learn. Training takes patience, persistence, and confidence. In time, you and your well-trained dog will have a solid foundation for a friendship based on mutual, loving respect.

Beyond Basic Training

Once your dog is trained in the basics, you are ready to try for a Canine Good Citizen certificate or to advance to obedience trials, agility, or another activity (see chapter 3, "The Sport of Dogs," and chapter 4, "You and Your Dog," for more on events and activities). You and your dog will benefit from the advanced vocabulary you can learn together as you hone your basic skills and learn new commands.

Glossary

Albino: A rare genetic condition resulting in white hair and pink eyes.

Almond eyes: Eyes shaped like almonds, rather than rounded.

Anterior: The front assembly of the body.

Apple head: A round-shaped skull.

Apron: Longer hair below the neck on the chest; also called the frill.

Articulation: Where two or more bones meet.

B

Bad mouth: Crooked teeth; when mouth is closed, upper and lower teeth do not line up according to the standard for the breed.

Balance: When all the parts of the dog moving or standing still produce a harmonious image.

Bandy legs: Legs that bend outward.

Bat ear: An ear that stands up, with a broad base, rounded at the top, with the opening facing forward.

Bay: The prolonged bark or voice of the hunting hound.

Beard: Thick, long hair on the underjaw.

Belton: A color pattern in English Setters (named after a village in England) made of ticking or roaning (see those entries in Glossary). Colors include blue belton (black and white), tricolor (blue belton with tan patches), orange belton (orange and white), lemon belton (lemon and white), and liver belton (liver and white).

Bench show: A dog show at which the dogs are kept on assigned benches when not in the show ring, so that interested people can view and learn more about them.

Bird dog: A sporting dog bred and trained to hunt game birds.

Bitch: A female dog.

Bite: The position of the upper and lower teeth when the mouth is closed. Bite positions include scissors, level, undershot, or overshot, depending on the breed.

Blaze: A white stripe running up the center of the face, usually between the eyes.

Blocky: Square or cube-like formation of the head.

Blue merle: A color pattern of black blotches or streaks on a blue-gray background. *See* Merle.

Bobtail: A dog born without a tail, or a dog with a tail docked very short. Often used as a name for the Old English Sheepdog.

Brace: Two of the same breed presented together as a pair.

Brindle: A color pattern in which black is layered over a lighter color (usually tan), producing a tiger-striped effect.

Broken-haired: A rough, wiry coat.

Brush: A bushy tail; a tail heavy with hair.

Bullbaiting: An ancient sport in which the dog tormented a bull.

Button ear: A small, neat ear with the flap folding forward, covering the opening of the ear.

C

Canid: A family (Canidae) of carnivorous animals including dogs, wolves, coyotes, foxes, and jackals.

Cape: Long, thick hair covering the shoulders.

Cat foot: Neat, round foot, with high-arched toes held closely together.

China eye: A clear or spotted blue, light blue, or whitish eye.

Choke collar: A leather or chain collar that tightens or loosens by the hand and leash.

Cobby: Compact, with a short body.

Condition: Health as shown by the coat, skin, general appearance, and behavior.

Conformation: The form and structure, make and shape; arrangement of the parts in conformance with breed standards.

Congenital: Present at birth; may have genetic or environmental causes.

Coursing: The sport of chasing prey with sighthounds.

Cropping: The cutting or trimming of ear leather to cause the ear to stand erect.

Cry: The baying or "music" of hounds.

Culotte: The longer hair on the back of the thighs.

D

Dam: The female parent.

Dapple: A splotchy or mottled coat color pattern.

Dewclaw: An extra claw on the inside of the leg; a vestigal fifth toe, removed on most breeds.

Digit: Toe.

Dish-faced: A slight concaveness of foreface when viewed in profile.

Disqualification: A decision made by a judge or committee that a dog has a condition making him ineligible for competition under the dog show rules or standard for his breed; or an undesirable feature of the dog that makes him ineligible for competition.

Dock: To shorten the tail by cutting.

Dog: A male dog; also used for male and female.

Dog show: A competitive exhibition for dogs in which the dogs are judged on conformation according to the established standard for the breed.

Domed: Evenly rounded in topskull; curved, not flat.

Double coat: An outer coat resistant to weather and protective against brush and brambles, with an undercoat of softer hair for warmth and waterproofing.

Drop ear: The ear leather folds over; not erect or prick ears.

Dudley nose: Flesh-colored

Expression: The general appearance of all features of the head.

Fall: Hair overhanging the face.

Fancier: A person especially interested and active in some phase of the sport of purebred dogs.

Fawn: A medium brown color.

Feathering: The longer fringe of hair on ears, legs, tail, or body.

Field trial: A competition of hounds or sporting breeds in which dogs are judged on ability and style in tracking, finding, or retrieving game.

Flag: A long tail, carried high. Feathering on tail.

Flush: To drive birds from cover, to force them to take flight; to spring.

Foxy: Sharp expression; pointed nose with short foreface.

Frill: *See* Apron.

Gait: The pattern of footsteps at various rates of speed, with a particular rhythm and footfall.

Game: Wild birds or animals that are hunted.

Gazehound: Greyhound or other sight-hunting hound.

Genealogy: Recorded family descent; pedigree.

Gestation: A period of 63 days in which the dog is pregnant with puppies.

Grizzle: A mixture of color including gray, black, and red hairs.

Groom: To brush, comb, trim, or otherwise make a dog's coat and appearance neat.

Gun dog: A dog trained to work with its master in finding live game and retrieving game that has been shot.

Hackles: Hairs on neck and back raised in fright or anger.

Hallmark: A trait of the dog that identifies his breed—for example, the spectacles of the Keeshond or the hackney-like action of the Miniature Pinscher.

Handler: A person hired to take the dog into the show ring or field trial.

Harlequin: Patched or pied coloration, usually black or gray on white.

Harness: A leather or cloth strap shaped around the shoulders and chest, with a ring at its top for the lead.

Haw: A third eyelid or membrane on the inside corner of the eye.

Inbreeding: The mating of closely related dogs of the same breed.

Interbreeding: The breeding of dogs of the same breed but different variety.

Kiss marks: Tan spots on the cheeks and over the eyes.

Lead: A strap, cord, or chain attached to the collar or harness; leash.

Line breeding: The mating of dogs of the same breed within the line or family, to a common ancestor; for example, a dog to his granddam.

Lion color: Tawny; a medium reddish-brown.

Liver: A dark brown color.

Lumbering: An awkward gait.

Mad dog: A dog with rabies.

Mane: Long, thick hair on top and sides of neck.

Mask: Dark shading on the foreface.

Merle: A color pattern of dark blotches against a lighter background of the same color, usually gray-blue.

Milk teeth: First teeth.

Mottled: Pattern of dark roundish blotches on a lighter background.

Music: The baying of hounds.

Muzzle: The head in front of the eyes: foreface, nose, and jaws.

Neuter: To perform a surgical operation on the dog's testicles to prevent fertilization of bitches.

Otter tail: Thick at the root, round, and tapering, with the hair parted or divided on the underside.

Pack: Several hounds kept together in one kennel. Mixed pack is made of males and females.

Pads: Shock-absorbing cushions on the underside of the feet. Soles.

Parti-color: Patches of a different color from the rest of the coat, in which there are individual hairs of at least one different color on a white base color.

Pedigree: The written record of a dog's genealogy of three generations or more.

Penciling: Black lines dividing the tan on the toes.

Peppering: The mixture of individual black and white hairs, not patches of separate colors, that give a sprinkling of salt-and-pepper effect.

Pied: Patches of white and another color.

Plume: A long fringe of hair on the tail; or carrying the tail plumelike over the back.

Poach: When hunting, to trespass on private property.

Point: The immovable stance of the hunting dog to indicate the presence and position of the game.

Police dog: Any dog trained for police work.

Pompon: A rounded tuft of hair on the end of the tail when the coat is clipped.

Prick ear: Ear carried erect, usually pointed at tip.

Puppy: A dog under twelve months of age.

Purebred: A dog whose sire and dam belong to the same breed, and are themselves of unmixed descent since recognition of the breed.

R

Racy: Appearing fast and agile, without any loss of substance.

Rangy: Tall, long in body, high on leg, light-framed; gangly.

Retrieve: A hunting term. The act of bringing back shot game to the handler.

Roan: A mixture of colored hairs with white hairs.

Ruff: Thick, longer hair growing around neck.

S

Saber tail: Carried in a semi-circle.

Sable: Coat color produced by black-tipped hairs on a background of silver, gold, gray, fawn, or brown.

Saddle: Variation of coat color over the back, like a saddle.

Sighthound: *See* Gazehound.

Sire: The male parent.

Sled dogs: Dogs worked, usually in teams, to pull sleds.

Spay: To perform a surgical operation on a bitch's ovaries to prevent conception of puppies.

Speak: To bark.

Spectacles: Shadings or dark markings over or around the eyes or from eyes to ears.

Splashed: Irregularly patched color on white, or white on color.

Spring: *See* Flush.

Square body: A dog whose measurements from withers to ground equals that from forechest to rump.

Stance: Way of standing.

Standard: A description of the ideal dog of each recognized breed, to serve as a word pattern by which dogs are judged at shows.

Stop: The step up from muzzle to back skull.

Stud book: A record of the breeding information of dogs of recognized breeds.

Stud dog: A male dog used for breeding purposes.

Substance: Solidity of body.

Symmetry: Pleasing balance among all parts of the dog.

Team: Usually four dogs exhibited by one handler.

Ticked: Small, isolated areas (smaller than spots) of black or colored hairs on a white background.

Topknot: A tuft of longer hair on top of the head.

Topline: The outline of the back from just behind the withers to the tail.

Trail: To hunt by following ground scent.

Tricolor: Three colors in the coat: white, black, and tan.

Trousers: Longish hair at the back of both upper and lower thighs.

Tulip ear: An ear carried erect with edges curving in and forward.

Webbed toes: Toes connected by a skin membrane; important for water-retrieving dogs, providing help in swimming.

Wheaten: Pale yellow or fawn color.

Wirehair: Having a coat of hard, crisp, wiry texture.

Withers: The region defined by the highest parts of the backbone (spine) and the shoulders; just below the neck and before the topline.

Index

first-aid kit, 241–42
Flat-Coated Retriever, 51
fleas, 227
food:
  for adult dogs, 222–23
  and elimination, 218
  and gastrointestinal problems,
    235–36, 239
  and housebreaking, 245
  and nutrition, 221, 222–23
  for puppies, 222, 223
  treats and supplements, 223
  types of, 222
  what to avoid in, 223
  when, how much, and how often to give,
    222–23
Foxhounds (American and English), 80,
  81
Fox Terriers (Smooth and Wire),
  128–29
fractures, 239
French Bulldog, 15, 181, 226, 245
friendliness, 5

games, and safety, 9
gas, excessive, 236
gastrointestinal problems, 235–36,
  239
Gazette, AKC, 13–14, 15
German Shepherd Dog, 204–5
German Shorthaired Pointer, 52
German Wirehaired Pointer, 27, 53,
  231
Giant Schnauzer, 103
glossary, 253–63
Golden Retriever, 7, 10, 14, 38, 54–55,
  219, 226
Gordon Setter, 56–57
Great Dane, 104
Greater Swiss Mountain Dog, 106
Great Pyrenees, 105
Greyhound, 82
grooming:
  anal sacs, 221
  and bathing, 220
  brushing, 219–20, 221
  cleaning ears, 221
  cleaning eyes, 221
  cleaning teeth, 221
  how-tos, 221
  nail trimming, 220, 221
  routine for, 219–21
  tools for, 220
Groups:
  at all-breed shows, 18, 19
  herding dogs, 191
  hounds, 69
  miscellaneous class, 211
  non-sporting dogs, 171
  sporting dogs, 39
  terriers, 119
  toy dogs, 147
  working dogs, 95
gums:
  healthy, 217, 221
  problems with, 235

hair:
  brushing of, 219–20, 221
  cleaning of, 221
  healthy, 216
  lice in, 227
  long or short, 6
  loss of, 228, 233
  shedding of, 6, 220, 221
Harrier, 83
Havanese, 212
head problems, 234
health, 7, 213–42
  and AKC Canine Health Foundation,
    12
  and appearance, 215–19
  artificial respiration, 238
  basic concerns, 215–23
  bleeding, 238, 240
  of body systems, 232–37
  of coat, 216
  congenital disorders, 231
  diarrhea, 239
  of ears, 216–17, 234

law, and dogs, 12–13
leash, for training, 247
length, measurement of, 36
Lhasa Apso, 183
library, AKC, 15–16
lice, 227
limping, 232, 234
liquid medicine, giving to your dog, 228
lost dogs, 12
Lowchen, 212
lumps or bumps, 233
lure coursing, 24
  titles in, 25, 26
Lyme disease, 227, 234, 236, 237

male dogs, 6, 18, 229
Maltese, 159
Manchester Terrier, 133
Manchester Terrier (Toy), 160
mange, 227–28
Mastiff, 109
mats, removing of, from coat, 221
measurement, of height and length, 36
medicine, giving to your dog, 228
mineral oil, in eyes, 220
Miniature Bull Terrier, 134
Miniature Pinscher, 161
Miniature Poodle, 184
Miniature Schnauzer, 135
miscellaneous class, 211–12
mischievous dogs, 5
mites, 227–28
mouth:
  healthy, 217, 221
  problems of, 234
multisystem problems, 237
musculoskeletal problems, 234
museum, 16
muzzle or restraint, in emergency, 237

nails, trimming of, 220, 221
nervous system problems, 236
neutering, 228–29

Newfoundland, 110
non-sporting dogs, 170–89
  list of, 171
Norfolk Terrier, 136
Norwegian Elkhound, 86
Norwich Terrier, 137
nose:
  healthy, 217
  problems of, 232, 233, 234
Novice Class:
  in all-breed show, 18
  in Junior Showmanship, 28
Novice work, obedience trials, 21
nutrition:
  and health, 221, 222–23
  and loss of appetite, 232
  treats and supplements, 223

obedience training, 246–52
  collar for, 246–47, 251
  come, 249–50, 252
  down, 248–49
  heel, 250–51
  praise in, 252
  sit, 247, 252
  stay, 248
  time commitment for, 246
  tips for, 251–52
obedience trials, 20–21
  titles in, 25, 26
ointment, applying, 228
Old English Sheepdog, 190, 206
Open class:
  all-breed show, 18
  in Junior Showmanship, 28
Open work, obedience trials, 21
Otterhound, 87
overweight dogs, 219

paint, poisoning from, 241
panting, difficulty in, 232
paper training, 245–46
Papillon, 162
paralysis, 236